LIFE ISSUES

ALCOHOLISM

by Chris Varley

Marshall Cavendish
NEW YORK • LONDON • TORONTO • SYDNEY

Published by Marshall Cavendish Corporation
2415 Jerusalem Avenue
North Bellmore, New York 11710
USA

Varley, Chris.
    Alcoholism/Chris Varley.
        p.   cm.—(Life Issues)
    Includes bibliographical references and index.
    Summary: Defines alcoholism and describes its causes, symptoms, and treatment.
        ISBN 1-85435-612-7
        1. Alcoholism—United States—Juvenile literature.   2. Drinking of alcoholic beverages—United States—
Juvenile literature.
    [1. Alcoholism.] I. Title. II. Series.
    HV5066. V37 1994
    382. 29'2'0973—dc20   93-23961
                                                                                                        CIP
                                                                                                        AC

Produced by The Creative Spark
Editor: Gregory Lee
Art direction: Robert Court
Design: Mary Francis-DeMarois, Robert Court
Page layout, graphic illustration: Elayne Roberts

Marshall Cavendish Editorial Director: Evelyn M. Fazio
Marshall Cavendish Editorial Consultant: Marylee Knowlton

Printed and bound in the United States

Photographic Note
Several persons depicted in this book are photographic models; their appearance in these photographs is solely to
dramatize some of the situations and choices facing readers of the Life Issues series.

Photo Credits
Christie Costanzo p. 4, 6, 8, 11, 12, 15, 18, 20, 29, 32, 33, 36, 39, 45, 46, 48, 51, 54, 58, 62, 66, 71, 72, 74, 76, 79, 82
PhotoEdit p. 26 (Elena Rooraid); 30, 57, 69 (Robert Brenner); 43 (Tony Freeman); 60 (David Young-Wolff);
            84 (James L. Shaffer)

Cover photo: Pedrick/The Image Works

Acknowledgments
*With the exception of the researchers and experts who have been identified and quoted as such, all names have been changed to
protect the identities of those people who were willing to share their stories for this book. Without their help, this book could
never have been written.*

Permission to use the "Middle School Contract for Life" granted by SADD National (Students Against Driving Drunk).

Special thanks to Irene Veralli-Gutmann, C.S.W., M.S.W.

TABLE OF CONTENTS

PROLOGUE

What is alcoholism? Can I catch it from somebody else? If I get drunk, does that make me an alcoholic? Can someone who is an alcoholic ever get better? What makes a person turn into an alcoholic in the first place?

These are just a few of the questions you may be asking yourself as you pick up this book. Even if you've never had a drink in your life, you probably know people who have. Chances are you may even know somebody who has a drinking problem. One out of every eight adults—and one out of every 15 teenagers—has a serious problem with alcohol. So it's only natural for you to be curious.

It's also natural for you to be confused. Alcoholism is a complicated subject. Even experts can't agree on whether alcoholism is a disease like cancer or diabetes, or whether it's a symptom of some deeper psychological problem.

Many doctors consider alcoholism to be a disease. They argue that alcoholism has symptoms, like a disease; that it gets progressively worse over time, like a disease; and that it can be fatal if not treated in time, just like a disease. For many people, however, the word "disease" conjures up frightening images. Many psychologists and sociologists feel that stereotyping a person as an "alcoholic" is both insulting and demeaning, and only encourages them to hide their drinking problem rather than deal with it. Other psychologists prefer to say that the person has a problem with alcohol addiction, alcohol dependence, or alcohol abuse. These terms focus attention on the effects of excessive drinking, rather than make moral judgments. Alcohol dependency and abuse are serious, debilitating conditions. They affect not only the drinker, but all those with whom he or she interacts. Even those who choose not to drink cannot entirely escape the effects of alcohol, since others around them drink—and often to excess.

Whether you are worried about the impact that other people's drinking could have on your life, about drinking habits of a friend or relative, or about your own drinking, this book will help you sort through the confusing and contradictory issues surrounding alcohol use and abuse. The more you know about alcohol and its effects, the better prepared you will be to make the right choices about drinking alcohol.

1

GETTING STARTED

My first experience getting drunk wasn't
like, you know, throwing up all over the
place and remembering that day forever. It
was just that I'd feel real comfortable getting buzzed.
—"Jeffrey," a recovering alcoholic

It all started innocently enough. Jordan, age eight, snuggled up in his father's lap in front of the fireplace. It was late, and he was sleepy, but this was Christmas and there was a party going on. To celebrate, Jordan's father let him have a taste of beer. Jordan didn't like it.

A few years later, when he was in eighth grade, Jordan helped out at a neighbor's high school graduation party. He and a buddy were allowed to be at the party if they agreed to clean up afterward. While they were cleaning, they came across the kegs used to serve beer. When no one was looking, they each took a drink—and then another. By the time Jordan finally staggered home well after midnight, he was, as he puts it, "plowed." By the time he was 16, Jordan had begun to drink regularly. He was aware that he sometimes abused alcohol, using it as an excuse to do things he wouldn't ordinarily do. "But I was in a huge state of denial. When you're in eighth, ninth, tenth grade, even college, you think you are untouchable. You never think that you're out of control. You never really believe you have

Drinking excessively is a major problem for millions of adults,
who often begin abusing alcohol when they are very young.

Social gatherings commonly feature alcohol for guests to enjoy. Alcoholics, however, cannot control their need to drink because they are addicted.

a problem with alcohol. You don't even understand the circumstances of how alcohol can affect you, how it can be bred into you, in your genes. How it can be learned. Or how it can be both."

It took Jordan 10 more years to finally face up to the fact that he had a drinking problem. He was starting to have problems at work and knew that he had to do something fast. It's been nearly three years since Jordan has had a drink. "I don't drink anymore because I choose not to. If I wanted to, I could choose to drink again, but I choose not to drink because it allows me to be in control. I may have a drink again someday, or I may never have another drink again. The choice is up to me."

Sooner or later everyone has to face the decision of whether or not to drink. For most people, the use of alcohol within a social setting never becomes a problem. They can have a drink or two with friends or a glass of wine with dinner without becoming drunk or belligerent. For some people, however, alcohol use turns into alcohol abuse. They can no longer control either their drinking or their behavior while under the influence of too much alcohol. What kind of people become alcoholics? What makes them turn into alcoholics?

Alcoholism is an addiction. An addiction is either a psychological or a physical dependence on something, usually (but not always) a drug. People who are psychologically addicted to alcohol often feel as if they just can't function without it. They "need" to drink to get through the day, or to ask that certain someone to dance with them. They are also frequently obsessed with alcohol, and are constantly looking for opportunities to drink more.

Physical addiction occurs over time as the body adjusts to the presence of alcohol in the system. When that alcohol is suddenly removed—when the addicted person is denied access to liquor—the person often experiences symptoms of withdrawal: body shakes or tremors, excessive perspiration, nausea, and vomiting. This occurs because the body, which has had years to adapt to the presence of alcohol in the system, must now suddenly readjust to its absence in a short period of time. In extreme cases of physical dependence, withdrawal may result in hallucinations and even death.

An alcoholic, then, is someone who is obsessed with alcohol, has an overwhelming and continuing urge to drink, and has a dependence on alcohol. Alcoholics can neither control how much they drink nor their actions while drinking, even though they may think they can. "I never drank until after five o'clock," remembers Ted, "so I thought I was the one who was in control of my drinking. The problem was, I could never not drink after five—so I really wasn't the one who was in control. The booze was."

WHAT IS ALCOHOLISM?

Alcoholism is characterized by both a psychological and a physical addiction to alcohol. Even though alcoholics know what will happen when they drink, they continue to do so anyway. Alcoholics are powerless to control their own lives. According to the National Council on Alcoholism, "The alcoholic has lost the power of choice in the matter of drinking....The alcoholic's body 'needs' alcohol to function."

An important feature of alcoholism is denial. Denial, the refusal to admit that a drinking problem even exists, is perhaps the single most significant obstacle to overcoming an alcohol-related problem. Most alcoholics fail to recognize that they are addicted—or even admit that they have a drinking problem—until after it has seriously damaged their lives and their health.

Another feature of alcoholism is that it is much harder to recognize than many people realize. The stereotype of a down-on-his-luck, drunken bum actually represents only a tiny fraction of alcoholics, no more than three or four percent. Most alcoholics lead what would appear to be fairly normal lives. They go to school or have jobs, get married, buy houses, and have children. At some point in their lives, however, alcohol becomes a problem. They begin to lose control over when and how they drink.

Robert is a good example. Like most people, he began experimenting with alcohol as a teenager, sneaking the odd drink here or there, and occasionally getting drunk at a party. Then he graduated, got a good job, married, and started a family. Because of his new responsibilities, he didn't drink as much as he had before—at least not at home. When his job required extensive travel, he started drinking more heavily. From the outside, his life appeared picture perfect: he had a good home and lots of money, and his children were doing well at private schools. Eventually, however, the drinking began taking its toll.

"Alcohol became the most important thing in my life," says Robert. "I lived to drink, and when I drank, I drank until I blacked out. I started arranging my life around my drinking."

Robert quit the company and started his own business. He was now free to drink whenever he wanted, and before long his drinking began taking the place of work. The business failed, and even though he didn't drink excessively at home, his marriage began to fall apart. His family became less important to him than his next drink. All of this happened before Robert was 30 years old.

Jeffrey's story is somewhat different. "The first time I tried alcohol was when I was nine years old," he recalls. "A friend of mine and I stole a couple of my dad's Olympias [a brand of beer] from the refrigerator because we just wanted to see what it was like, what it tasted like, and why adults liked to drink it. It was really nasty. I don't think I finished the whole thing. In fact, I know I didn't, because nothing happened to me." Four years passed before Jeffrey tried alcohol again. "It was still the curiosity issue," he says. "I wanted to understand why people got drunk, what it was about alcohol that made it such a social thing. My eighth grade graduation was coming up, and I thought it would be fun to cop a buzz. Somehow I got hold of three beers, drank one or two of them, and put the other in my bag with all my swimming stuff for the party after graduation. But my mom found out somehow and wouldn't let me go, so I was buzzed with nowhere to go."

Within a year Jeffrey found plenty of places to go. He was drinking before, during, and after parties and football games. "You just didn't go to a football game without being under the influence of something," he says. His grades began to slip, and he started withdrawing from other activities. By the time he entered college, he was, as he puts it, "really just floundering around. I couldn't really decide what to do with my life. I just wanted to get high and drink all the time."

Eventually Jeffrey's mother convinced him to get into a treatment program. He was diagnosed with having organic brain damage—a result of his drug and alcohol abuse. "When I heard that, it kind of scared me," Jeffrey remembers. "You know, when you're a kid you think, ' That'll never happen to me,' and then to hear that I might actually be permanently damaged and not even know it was pretty scary." It isn't necessary to be an alcoholic to have a drinking problem. In fact, it isn't even necessary to drink at all; the effects of alcohol are sometimes subtle and indirect and can cause as much damage to the lives of those around the drinker as the drinker himself.

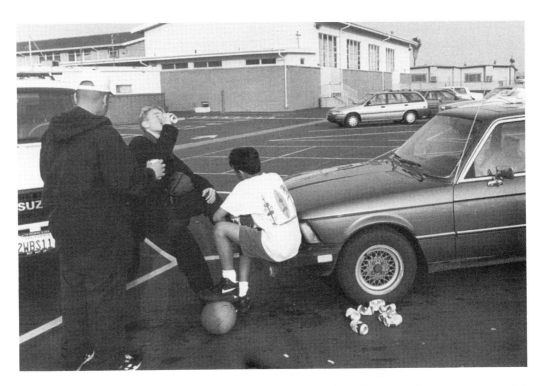

Many teenagers start drinking heavily with their friends. To gain acceptance with their peers, kids get together at concerts, sporting events, and parties to drink as much as possible.

John doesn't have a drinking problem, and he isn't an alcoholic, but his father was. "We knew by the way Dad came in the driveway what the rest of the evening was going to be like," he remembers. "We had a gravel driveway, so you could hear how fast his car was coming, and listen to it slide and bump along. Sometimes he'd even slam into the mailbox. We went through a lot of mailboxes. My sister was usually the lookout. She'd shout, 'Dad's home!' and we'd all run upstairs to our rooms." John hated to be around his father. "I don't think I ever saw my father sober," he recalls painfully. "Dinners were real gut-wrenchers. Rarely did we ever finish a dinner without one of us—me, or my sister, or my brother—getting mad and running up to our room. Mom would bring us our dinner later, play the peacemaker."

As a boy, John escaped his father's drinking by locking himself in his room and building model airplanes, fantasizing about being a pilot someday. When he was old enough to drive, he would often take the car after his father came home and drive out to the airport. "I'd just sit there and watch the planes taking off, and dream about flying away somewhere someday."

Eventually that's exactly what he did—by becoming a commercial airline pilot. His experiences as a child growing up with an alcoholic father, however, left him emotionally scarred.

Bars dispense alcohol like restaurants serve food. Some people are able to treat drinking as an activity that accompanies eating. Alcoholics, however, have lost any ability to moderate their drinking, and use it like a drug.

Children of alcoholics often suffer serious psychological damage as a result of their exposure to an alcoholic parent. They frequently have problems communicating with others, and usually have low self-esteem, or a poor opinion of themselves. Sometimes they try to compensate for their lack of self-esteem by criticizing the behavior of others.

John, for example, admits to having a poor sense of his own worth, and to being overly critical of other people. "I'm always telling everyone the right way to do things, trying to be in control of the situation. I know it's wrong, but I can't stop myself." Things got so bad at home that one of John's sons ran away to escape the constant criticism. As his son recalls, "I didn't realize it at the time, but a lot of the problems I had with my father were the result of my granddad's drinking."

WHY PEOPLE DRINK

If alcohol is the cause of so many problems in people's lives, why do they drink alcohol in the first place?

A lot of people say they drink alcohol because they like the taste. Jeffrey, however, remembers his first taste of alcohol as being "really nasty." In fact, most people who claim they like to drink because of the taste remember not liking it when they first tried it. How can this be?

Like olives or garlic or anchovies, alcohol is an acquired taste. Not everyone likes the way it tastes at first, but after trying it a few more times they get used to it. Certain kinds of alcohol might taste good with certain kinds of food—like beer with pizza, or red wine with steak or spaghetti. The taste of alcohol is enjoyed in the same way as the taste of food.

Not everyone, however, drinks because they like the taste. They drink because they like the way it makes them feel. It relaxes them, making them feel more comfortable and less tense. This effect is what can lead to a dependence upon alcohol—its relaxing effect. When pressed, some people may admit they drink to escape their problems. They are unable to cope with life without alcohol. This was the case with Jennifer's parents, and it quickly became the case with her as well. "I started taking liquor out of their liquor cabinet because I saw that was how my parents relaxed, how they dealt with problems," she says. "I remember being very young and thinking life is difficult, life is painful. I felt I deserved to take it easy. I really needed something to take the edge off. So I tried alcohol and it worked—for awhile."

Many teenagers use alcohol as a way to cope with their problems. One of the interesting properties of alcohol is its ability to relieve pain. Under the influence of alcohol, both physical and emotional pain often seem to disappear—at least temporarily. In fact, before the development of modern anesthesia, alcohol was often used to help patients get through the pain of a surgical operation (an anesthetic is any substance that produces a loss of sensation). Unfortunately, alcohol only masks the pain.

People who begin drinking as a way of dealing with problems in their lives find that alcohol doesn't solve anything. It just becomes another problem, and keeps them from dealing realistically with their other difficulties. Shortly after she began drinking, Jennifer found herself waking up in the morning craving beer. "It scared the hell out of me," she recalls, "because I didn't want to be like my parents. But I really wanted a drink bad. And when I did drink, I always overshot the mark. It was either not enough or too much. Either I wanted to get even more drunk, or I had already overshot the mark and I was throwing up. I was out of control."

Teenagers often start drinking because they think it's cool or because it makes them feel more grown up. Karen, a recovering alcoholic, says this is why she started. "It made me feel important. I liked the attention I got from the adults and from the other kids."

Many psychologists believe this need to look cool or get attention stems from some deeper problem such as low self-esteem. Those who drink because they want to look cool on the outside don't feel cool on the inside. They often feel their parents don't love them or understand them, or that they don't fit in with the rest of the crowd. Karen got drunk for the first time when she was 10. She was at a party with her mother. "The adults started giving me drinks," she remembers. "I liked all the attention I was getting; it was pretty neat. I just kept drinking and drinking because they kept giving it to me, so I got drunk. My mom thought it was cute. The next day I had a hangover [the headache and nausea that often occur after a bout of heavy drinking], so I didn't go to school. I thought it was really impressive telling all my friends why I missed school."

Just like taste, though, reasons for drinking often change over time. Karen soon found she was drinking not to look cool, but to escape the pain of living with an alcoholic mother. When her mother drank she would often become abusive toward Karen, both physically and verbally. Karen's mother married and divorced five times, and Karen said she had more brothers and sisters and stepbrothers and stepsisters than she could count. She often felt unloved and lost in the shuffle of her mother's life. "I tried running away about a dozen times, but that didn't work," she says. "So I just started drinking more instead."

At first she drank just at parties on the weekend, but then she began drinking during the week, to "practice" for the parties. "The more I drank, the more I was able to drink," she explains. "By the time I was in seventh grade, I was drinking every day. A friend of mine and I would split a case of beer [24 bottles] every day." The hangover she used to get after drinking disappeared because she was never sober long enough to get one. In order to get the alcohol she needed, Karen started hanging out with older kids. She would often trade sexual favors for booze. This only made her feel worse about herself and her life, and she began to drink even more to cover the pain.

WHERE IT ALL BEGINS

Exposure to alcohol begins at a very early age. Some children are introduced to alcohol before they are able to walk or talk. Parents might rub a small amount of whiskey on a teething baby's gums, for example, relying on the anesthetic properties of the alcohol to help soothe the baby's pain. Nursing mothers who drink pass the alcohol on to their babies through their breast milk. As children grow older, they see their parents drinking at parties and with meals. On television they see advertisements for beer and wine.

Children, teenagers, and adults alike are bombarded every day with commercials and advertising messages touting the good times to be had by drinking alcohol.

Although these first exposures to alcohol are often forgotten, there comes a time when children become consciously aware of alcohol and its implications. Karen remembers being four or five years old and seeing her mother drink. Occasionally her mother would let her have little sips. "I thought it was a privilege to sip my mom's drink," she says. "It made me feel very adult."

Jennifer was eight before she began to notice people drank but, unlike Karen, she remembers it as "something bad. People got a little out of control and used it to put a wall up between them and other people. It was a way to feel comfortable when you weren't comfortable."

Jordan first remembers realizing his parents drank when he was six years old. "I was in the back seat of my mother's gold Galaxy convertible," he recalls. "My father was ramming the car from behind with his Cadillac. Mom was screaming at him. It all started as a game, I think. We were coming home from a party, and he just kind of bumped our car a little at the stop light. Then he really stepped on the gas. They were both really drunk. I was scared for my life. I thought I was going to die."

GO ON, HAVE A DRINK!

In many cultures, drinking alcohol is a major and accepted form of socializing— a way of interacting with others. For example, business is conducted over martinis; weddings and holidays are celebrated with champagne; college parties often center on kegs of beer; and birthdays and promotions are celebrated with alcohol. Many bars offer a "Happy Hour" every day. Waiters or waitresses in restaurants will often ask before taking a food order, "Would you care for something from the bar?" A lot of sports fans think a Sunday afternoon football game is incomplete without beer.

Drinking and occasional drunkenness are often tolerated and sometimes even encouraged in our society, but not all drinking or all drunkenness. Drinking and driving is illegal. Underage drinking is illegal. Public drunkenness is also illegal, although few people are ever arrested for it unless their behavior creates a problem such as a fight or property damage.

Advertisements for alcohol enhance the image of drinking as something glamorous and fun. Liquor ads usually show people having a good time at a party or celebration, and frequently show men impressing attractive women by ordering the right kind of drink.

In one holiday ad for J & B Scotch, the words "ingle ells, ingle ells" appear, along with the question, "What would the holiday be without J & B?" "Think about what this is saying to us," says Dr. Marc Kern, a specialist in helping people recover from alcohol and other addictions. "It's saying that the holidays are meaningless unless you drink their booze." Some ads encourage people to drink while others, like those paid for by MADD (Mothers Against Drunk Driving),

WHEN IN ROME...

How big a role do cultural factors play in the development of alcoholism? Why do Mediterranean cultures, where wine is often consumed heavily, have lower rates of alcoholism than many European cultures? Perhaps part of the answer can be found in the way a culture uses alcohol.

Drunkenness is frowned upon in Jewish communities, for example, and the rate of alcoholism among Jews is very low. In Italy, wine is consumed almost exclusively with food at mealtime. It is treated as part of the meal. In France, where wine is popular both with meals and at other times of day, alcohol-related problems such as cirrhosis (a serious disease of the liver) occur frequently. In Ireland, where the alcoholism rate is very high, stealing a drink of whiskey from dad's bottle is often seen as a sign of independence. Being able to get away with it by replacing it with water demonstrates cleverness. In the United States, Americans are encouraged to do things with great gusto—to live life to its fullest. Unfortunately, this spills over into the consumption of alcohol.

Researchers have come up with a subtle but culturally significant difference between French and the American alcoholics: French alcoholics drink too much, are addicted to drinking, and suffer the physical ill effects just as Americans do, but their abuse of alcohol is more consistent and less disruptive of daily life. American alcoholics often drink massive quantities of liquor and become abusive and belligerent; then they may not drink at all for a short period of time. Soon, however, they will go at it again, drinking for the sake of drinking. Yet both types of drinkers are considered to be true alcoholics.

Many of these same researchers point out another interesting cultural difference: Jewish and Mediterranean cultures encourage stronger group associations than do European and American cultures. Americans encourage independence— not relying on others for help or support. Could it be that this attitude actually encourages the feelings of inadequacy and loneliness reported by many alcoholics as their reason for drinking?

discourage drinking. Sports heroes endorse certain brands of alcohol, while others encourage people to drink "responsibly." Is it any wonder, then, that so many people are confused about the difference between alcohol use and alcohol abuse?

Even religions present confusing messages about alcohol. Wine is used in Roman Catholic and other Christian churches as part of the ceremony of Communion, but the amounts consumed are so small that it would be impossible for someone to become drunk. On the other hand, some Christian denominations consider any use of alcohol to be wrong.

The Bible refers to Jesus turning water into wine for a wedding celebration at Canaan; but it also contains numerous negative references to drunkenness and

When people want to celebrate a special event, they often raise glasses of alcohol in a toast. This makes the use of alcohol something unique and desirable, even though it may have harmful consequences.

warns in Proverbs, "Be not among the winebibbers [heavy drinkers] or among gluttonous eaters of meat, for the drunkard and the glutton will come to poverty." The Koran prohibits the use of alcohol altogether, as do certain (but not all) Buddhist sects.

Another confusing message about alcohol comes from the way in which drunkenness is treated in movies and on television. While Sam the bartender on the TV show *Cheers* is a recovering alcoholic and doesn't drink, Norm sits at the bar and drinks all day without any ill effects. He's a popular and fun guy to be around.

To celebrate special occasions, people offer toasts to each other by clinking glasses together and drinking alcohol. This marks the event as a celebration, even though the beverage of choice isn't necessarily a good and healthy thing.

Lots of comedians make jokes about being drunk. W.C. Fields, Dean Martin, and Richard Pryor all built their careers as comedians around routines about drunkenness. Americans like to laugh at the silly things people do when they are drunk, but it's only make-believe drunken behavior that receives the laughter and applause of the audience. In real life, the serious problem of alcoholism often gets overlooked. For the person addicted to alcohol, the consequences of these attitudes are often a lifetime of severe emotional and physical pain.

2

THE GOOD, THE BAD, AND THE UGLY

Candy is dandy but liquor is quicker.
—Ogden Nash

Jennifer was 13 when she had her first "real" drink; Karen was only eight. They both had different reasons for drinking, and very different reactions, yet each of them eventually became an alcoholic. "I fixed a huge mixed drink for myself from my parents' liquor cabinet," Jennifer recalls. "I put a little bit of everything in it. I didn't really know what the different brands were. I put in some soda, too, and some ice. Then I sat in my room by myself and drank it. I liked the effects right away. It worked. The pain I felt [from being abused by her parents] went away. I wasn't doing it with friends and I wasn't doing it to be cool, I was just doing it to feel better, and it worked."

Karen remembers having her first drink on New Year's Eve, after her mother had gotten drunk and gone to bed. "She told my little brother and me that we could have anything we wanted, so my brother fixed us each a screwdriver. He knew how to make them from watching my mom, I guess. I don't remember how it tasted but I remember thinking it was pretty cool that my brother knew how to make a drink and that we were drinking. We both drank a couple of them, but I don't think I got drunk. Maybe he didn't make them right. I don't know. I just remember telling my brother that

Teenage drinking often starts here, with kids helping themselves to liquor at home while their parents are not around.

I didn't want to drink anymore because I didn't want to get sick like my mom. Which is funny, because that's exactly what I did anyway just a couple of years later."

WHAT IS ALCOHOL, ANYWAY?

Alcohol affects different people differently. It can even affect the same person in different ways at different times. Regardless of why a person starts to drink or how it affects them at first, however, the results of too much alcohol are often tragically the same. Those first few innocent, fun drinks can very easily evolve over time into a frightening and harmful addiction.

To understand how a person becomes addicted to alcohol, we need to know what alcohol is. The kind of alcohol that people drink is ethyl alcohol. Ethyl alcohol is very different from, say, rubbing alcohol (isopropyl alcohol). Isopropyl alcohol is a solvent that can be a deadly poison if taken into the body. It is not a food and has no food value. Ethyl alcohol, on the other hand, is both a food and a drug, a naturally occurring by-product of fermentation.

Fermentation is the process by which sugar is converted into carbon dioxide and alcohol due to the addition of yeast. Different types of alcohol, like wine, beer, and "hard" or distilled liquor contain varied concentrations of alcohol. As a result, not all alcoholic beverages are created equal. Most beers contain between

DRINK EQUIVALENCY

3-7%   10-14%   40-75%

12 oz. beer = 5 oz. wine = 1 1/2 oz. hard liquor (whiskey, rum, gin, etc.)

While different types of liquor contain different percentages of alcohol, most alcoholic drinks are served in varying portions so that the alcoholic content is proportionally the same for different drinks.

three and seven percent alcohol. Most wines, on the other hand, contain between 12 and 14 percent alcohol. Distilled liquor such as rum, gin, and whiskey can contain between 40 and 75 percent alcohol. The alcohol content of distilled spirits is most often referred to as the liquor's proof, which is equal to two times its alcohol content. A bottle of 80 proof scotch, for example, would contain 40 percent alcohol. Most alcoholic drinks, on the other hand, are created equal. As shown in the chart on page 22, the traditional drink serving sizes that have developed over time each contain roughly the same amount of alcohol. One 12-ounce beer—a standard-sized can or bottle—has the same amount of alcohol as a five-ounce glass of wine or a 1.5-ounce shot of hard liquor (whiskey, gin, vodka, rum, etc.).

Because of the effect alcohol has on the brain and central nervous system, alcohol is considered a drug. In fact, alcohol has been used as a medicine for centuries. In the thirteenth century, alcohol was believed to be a magical cure-all, even a means of attaining immortality. The image of a trustworthy St. Bernard dog with a small cask of brandy hanging around its neck being sent out to find and help lost skiers is based on fact; for many years alcohol was believed to be good for frostbite and other cold-related ills.

As late as the Civil War, alcohol was used to cleanse soldiers' wounds and help them endure the pain of battlefield surgery. The medical use of alcohol continues today; it can be found in many liquid cold remedies and mouthwashes.

Both as a food and as a drug, there can be no denying that for many people, drinking alcohol produces pleasurable sensations. The problem is that too much alcohol can and often does produce bad sensations along with the good. Alcohol is a sedative or a depressant. A sedative is a drug that inhibits or blocks certain nervous responses, thus "depressing" normal body functions.

One of the first functions alcohol depresses is the brain's ability to utilize oxygen in the bloodstream. This is why some people feel lightheaded or giddy when they drink; their brains are literally not getting enough oxygen. Because the brain's pain receptors are also depressed in the process, the experience feels pleasurable instead of painful.

As more alcohol is consumed, more of the brain's normal functions are depressed. A person who drinks a lot of alcohol in a short time experiences dizziness and a lack of physical coordination. Walking, talking, thinking things through, and making decisions all become more difficult with each successive drink. Just as a 13 or 14 percent concentration of alcohol is sufficient to kill the yeast that made the alcohol in the first place, a large enough concentration of alcohol in the human bloodstream can also prove fatal.

Unlike yeast, though, humans are able to tolerate only a small percentage of alcohol in their bodies. The presence of as little as 0.4 percent alcohol in the bloodstream is enough to produce a condition known as alcohol poisoning, which can lead to coma or even death.

The sedative effect of alcohol is potentially addictive. If it were not, alcoholism might be less of a problem than it is today. One peculiar aspect of sedatives is what is sometimes called their rebound or second-stage effects. Instead of the body returning to normal as the depressant wears off, a person will instead experience a sharp increase in brain and nervous system activity. This period can last up to 12 hours after drinking as little as one large drink.

In human terms, the result all too often goes something like this. Dad comes home from a hard day at the office. He has a drink to relieve his tension and anxiety. It works for a couple of hours, but then the second-stage sedative effects of the alcohol kick in. Suddenly he finds himself even more tense and anxious than he was before. Because he believes the first drink helped him relax, he wants another drink. What he doesn't realize is that the increased tension is a side effect of the earlier drink. So alcohol can actually increase—not decrease—a person's feelings of tension and anxiety.

Over time, alcohol can have a debilitating effect on the body as well as the mind. It has been implicated in cancer and other diseases of the stomach, pancreas, breast, and liver. When combined with smoking, alcohol produces an increased risk of cancer in the throat, tongue, and larynx.

Alcohol taken in large quantities and over a long period of time weakens the muscles and can cause them to atrophy, or waste away. At first the symptoms are relatively mild and may go unnoticed, but in time they can become quite painful. Many chronic alcoholics experience severe swelling and cramping in the legs. When this happens, a vicious cycle usually sets in. Because alcohol can help relieve the pain, these people begin drinking even more heavily. What they may not realize is that their drinking caused the pain in the first place.

John, whose father died from alcohol-related liver cancer, remembers watching his father's health slowly decline. "His stomach got really bloated because his liver was so swollen. His skin was all blotchy and scaly. If he sat too long, his legs would swell and cramp, but if he tried to move around, he didn't have the strength to walk or lift his arm without it hurting. So he'd have a drink—he'd have a whole bunch of drinks—and then the pain would go away for awhile, and he could move again, except that he was too drunk to do anything except sit there and stare at the TV. That's how he died, lying there in bed, drunk, watching TV and screaming about how much pain he was in."

If abused, any drug can have harmful effects. Alcohol is no exception. But in the right amount, at the right time, and for the right reason, drugs can also help people live better, healthier, richer lives. Is this also true of alcohol? Recent studies have indicated that there may indeed be healthful benefits derived from drinking alcohol, in moderation. Just what does "moderate" mean? In a recent study, moderation was defined as no more than one or two drinks per day, on average, for adults. Because alcohol physically affects teenagers differently than it does adults, the same study did not define any level of "moderate" consumption for teens.

REBOUND CHART

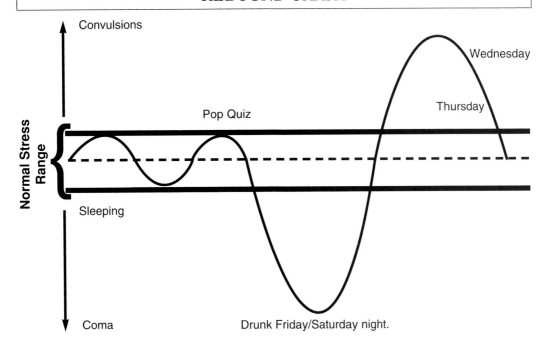

Every drug we put in our bodies produces specific biochemical reactions. This chart shows a person's normal stress range, from the state of sleep to the anxiety and alertness of taking a test at school. The dotted line is the average stress level when awake. When we consume alcohol—a depressant—it slows the body down, below its normal stress range. This is the relaxing effect people feel when they drink, for example, at a weekend party. They may act boisterously for a few hours because alcohol suppresses judgment and our normal inhibitions, but a few hours later the sedative effect will lead to unconsciousness.

Since alcohol is a strong drug, it takes longer for the body to recover and purge itself of the alcohol. All drugs create rebound effects, where the body balances itself by having an opposite reaction to the initial effect. In this case, the drunkeness of the weekend turns into a highly stressful, post-weekend funk that many people blame on their job or their teacher or their spouse, but the source of tension is not necessarily their environment but the drug they've been taking. The rebound effect of alcohol is making them feel irritated and anxious, but many people who abuse it do not make the connection. As the week progresses, the body eventually begins to return to its normal stress range, when the cycle will start to repeat itself.

Drugs like cocaine also have rebound effects, but cocaine works in just the opposite way: the initial "high" makes the user euphoric, while the subsequent low or "crash" is extreme depression. Caffeine in coffee has a similar effect, but because it is far less powerful, the effects are felt over the course of a few hours instead of days.

Overindulgence of alcohol can lead to coma and death; other drugs like cocaine can produce heart attacks and convulsions that also lead to death.

One expert suggested that if there is any safe level of drinking for teenagers approaching adulthood, it is no more than one or two drinks per month. Alcohol does relieve stress. In moderation, alcohol also seems to increase levels of HDL, or so-called "good" cholesterol in the bloodstream. Some studies have shown that moderate amounts of dry, non-sweet wines or distilled spirits diluted with water may be helpful in the treatment of diabetes. While people who are heavy drinkers die at a significantly higher rate than do non-drinkers, people who drink moderately appear to live longer than people who don't drink at all.

Researchers of the study cited above were careful to point out that by "on average" they didn't mean a person could drink a six-pack on Saturday, nothing else the rest of the week, and average it out to one drink a day. They meant no more than one or two drinks a day, period. Drinking more than this eliminates any health benefits that might otherwise be associated with moderate drinking, and remember, this is for adults, not teens.

DISEASE AND ALCOHOL

Unlike other drugs, a prescription isn't needed to buy or use alcohol. As a result, the health benefits of alcohol may be best considered by looking at it as a food. In the same way that moderating daily intake of saturated fats helps reduce the risk of certain kinds of heart disease, the moderate intake of alcohol—as a part of the diet—may have beneficial effects on one's health. It is important to remember, however, that there are better ways of improving your health than by drinking alcohol. Eating less fat and getting plenty of exercise will increase the levels of HDL in your blood and reduce your risk of heart disemuch more efficiently than alcohol, and without any of the negative side effects associated with drinking. Even moderate drinking apparently causes some damage to the body and puts the drinker at a greater risk for developing certain diseases such as breast cancer. The harm that alcohol can cause to the body of a young person far outweighs any potential health benefits.

There are many substances besides alcohol that affect young people differently than adults. For example, the health benefits of aspirin are well known in adults, and yet aspirin has been implicated in the development of Reye's Syndrome—a very serious disease—in young people.

Some laboratory studies seem to confirm that a modest amount of alcohol consumption helps maintain a healthier level of HDL—"good" cholesterol. But experience teaches us that too much alcohol is bad for the body, and can cause many problems for organs such as the liver. Many doctors do not like to promote the so-called "healthy" aspects of alcohol consumption for fear that it will encourage drinking to excess.

THAT'S NOT THE WAY I SEE IT

Along with depressing levels of tension and anxiety in the brain, alcohol also interferes with the drinker's perception of reality. Under the influence of alcohol, many people become less inhibited. After a few drinks, they feel quite comfortable doing things they might not otherwise do, because they were too embarrassed or shy or "knew better."

Jeffrey, profiled earlier in this book, first began drinking out of curiosity. Soon, however, he discovered that drinking "allowed" him to do things he was too shy to do otherwise, like ask a girl to dance at a party. "I found out that by drinking beers in social situations, like at football games or dances, it broke down a lot of the barriers," he recalls. "It made me feel loose, made it easier for me to talk to people and meet girls. The first year of high school, you're surrounded by all these new people and drinking helps take away some of the fear."

This may help explain the popularity of drinking as a social activity. The increase in sociability may really be due to a lowering of inhibitions, but it may also be due in part to the belief that alcohol helps improve sociability. If a person believes that a drug will affect them in a certain way, he (or she) will usually act that way, even when he isn't taking the drug. This is called the placebo effect. In one study, a group of people were told they were being served alcohol, when they were really being served nonalcoholic beverages. As the evening progressed, these people acted as if they were becoming drunk and more sociable.

Not all the effects of drinking alcohol can be attributed to the placebo effect, however. Alcohol really does change a drinker's perception of reality. Many drinkers report feeling more handsome or beautiful, stronger, and even more popular when they drink. In fact, none of these things are true. If anything, they probably become less attractive, weaker, and less popular. Because of the effect of alcohol on their perception, they just see things differently. Objective tests of strength and reflex control reveal that no one under the influence of alcohol is able to react or perform as well as when they are sober.

DRIVING UNDER THE INFLUENCE

Changes in perception play a major role in driving under the influence of alcohol. Many teens say that drinking makes them feel more adult. Driving a car also makes them feel more adult, but the combination of drinking and driving keeps many teens from ever becoming adults. Nearly one-half of all fatal auto accidents can be attributed to driving while under the influence of alcohol. Worse, while teenagers make up only about 17 percent of the driving population, they are at fault in more than 35 percent of alcohol-related accidents.

The brain's ability to process information such as speed, distance, the curve of the road, and even the difference between the gas pedal and the brake

Fatal auto accidents involving alcohol prove that drinking and driving don't mix.

becomes impaired while drinking. Gone, too, is the brain's ability to recognize that these functions have been impaired. Drivers who have been videotaped while performing roadside sobriety tests are often later amazed at how badly they did.

"I felt sure I wasn't drunk. There was no way I was drunk. I clearly passed the test," said one such driver. "These guys were just taking me in because they just wanted to bust my chops. They didn't like me, that was all. But then when I saw the tape the next morning, I couldn't believe it. That 'straight line' I walked weaved all over the place. I even fell down in the middle of it, and I still don't remember doing that. And I was acting like such a jerk." Tim, a recovering alcoholic, reports having several DUI (Driving Under the Influence) arrests before he turned 18. After one, a small fender bender, he panicked and ran—leading police on a city-wide chase that ended with him being surrounded by police with their guns drawn.

Jennifer also remembers having a traffic accident while drunk, then fleeing the scene. "That was so unlike me," she says. "I'm not that kind of person. It was just totally out of character, but my head was not functioning, and it seemed like a good idea at the time."

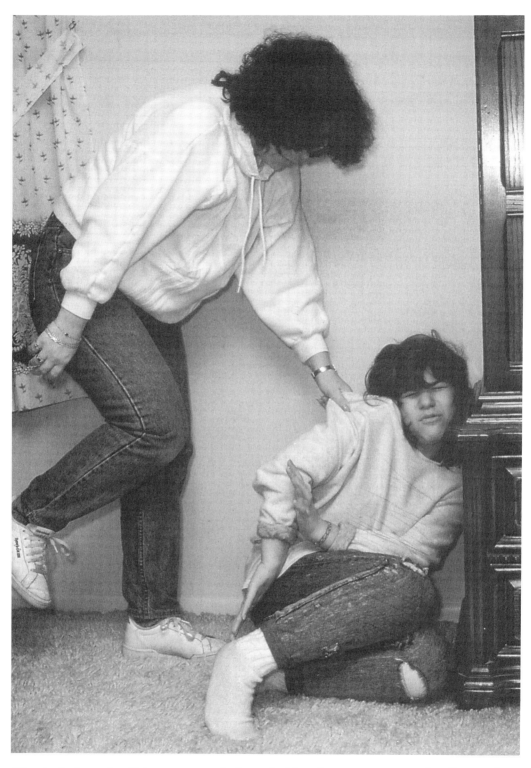

Physical abuse is all too common in households where one or more family members are alcoholic.

A BAD INFLUENCE

Drinking frequently brings out feelings of anger and hostility that have otherwise been kept under control. Nearly one-half of all murders in this country occur while either the attacker or his victim—or both—are under the influence of alcohol. Recent statistics reveal that more than one-half of the college students accused of violent crimes were either drinking or taking drugs at the time of their crime. Nearly one-half of their victims also reported having been either drunk or high when the attack occurred.

Alcohol plays a major role in many cases of child and spouse abuse, and is also a significant factor in many suicides. Often people who know better when they are sober will, under the influence of alcohol, become so depressed and confused that they believe hurting someone close to them or killing themselves is the only solution to their problems. Their judgment has become so clouded and impaired that they are no longer able to make the right decision or take the appropriate action. Their every emotion is pushed and stretched to the breaking point.

What is it about alcohol that brings out the beast in some people? Many psychologists believe that acting out extremes of socially unacceptable behavior while under the influence of alcohol is how some people try to cope with their own feelings of inferiority or powerlessness. What some people perceive as tension and anxiety often stems from feelings of inadequacy or hopelessness. They believe they aren't "good enough," and drink to relieve their tension—thereby depressing their inhibitions and releasing "the demons" locked up inside. Most recovering alcoholics appear to verify this, citing intense feelings of self-loathing and worthlessness as key components of their drinking.

Jeffrey began drinking out of curiosity, but soon found that drinking was a way to deal with the pressure he felt from his father to "make something" of himself. "The fear of failure was everything," he recalls. "There was all this pressure. It was too much." It all got to be too much, Jeffrey admits, because he felt he wasn't good enough to do it. He couldn't live up to his father's standards. He had no self-esteem.

Donald began drinking for similar reasons. Growing up gay in a conservative middle-class family, he often felt worthless and bad. "I knew I was different from everybody else and I knew everybody thought it was wrong and sick and I couldn't handle it. Part of me thought it was sick, too. So I would go out and get drunk, and if I was with my friends, we'd beat up on some queers, and I always beat them the hardest, to prove I wasn't really gay."

Pat remembers being in college, and feeling lots of pressure from her parents to achieve. "But everyone else there was so much smarter than I was, so much better. They deserved to be there, I didn't. I didn't know why they let me in." When Pat started drinking with friends she found these feelings of inadequacy would come to the surface. Inevitably she would wind up drunk,

sprawled out on the ground in front of her dormitory and unable to find her key and let herself in. She would just lie there on the ground, wailing and sobbing, until someone came down and helped her up to her room.

MOOD SWINGS

Why does someone continue to drink if it makes them feel so bad? George Vaillant, a researcher at Harvard University, suggests that the kind of anxiety and tension alcohol relieves best is the very anxiety and tension that builds up the most while someone is temporarily not drinking. "Small amounts of alcohol may briefly change mood for the better; larger amounts of alcohol may reduce guilt, [and] release behavior usually suppressed by punishment." The person drinks, gets their "bad feelings" out of their system, sobers up, and finds suddenly that they feel even worse about themselves. This is very similar to the rebound effect of sedatives: drinking relieves the tension at first, then causes it to increase later as the effects begin to wear off.

As a result, males who have feelings of inferiority may start fights while drinking to prove how tough they are. Then, feeling even more inferior for behaving so badly, they get stuck in a vicious cycle of drinking and fighting as a way of coping with feelings of inferiority. Females, especially in the teen years, wrestle with issues related to sex and the development of their bodies. They may use alcohol as an excuse to act sexually contrary to their normal behavior. Those who feel powerless in their jobs or relationships may feel more powerful while drunk, and verbally abuse others or get into fights. They might beat members of their family or even rape someone. Then, feeling powerless to do anything to ease the pain they've caused, they will continue to drink and commit the same offenses.

Such behavior isn't just limited to alcoholics; it can occur in anyone who abuses alcohol. Paul reports one occasion where, after drinking heavily, he got in a fight with his wife and hit her. "I'd been going through a very rough time. My first wife had died a couple of years before. I felt guilty about that, even though there wasn't anything I could do about it. She'd had a heart attack. But I felt guilty because I was still alive, and she wasn't. And now I was married to someone else, and it wasn't the same. It wasn't working out, and we were arguing, and I hit her. It was the first time and the last time. The marriage broke up after that." Even though Paul isn't an alcoholic, he did have a problem with alcohol when he tried to use it to deal with his guilt and anger.

BUT WE'RE HAVING SUCH A GOOD TIME!

Some people are "happy drunks." They laugh, are friendly, and have a good time. They don't cause any trouble, so what's wrong with drinking if it makes them feel silly?

Some people experience rapid mood swings, from "happy drunk" (see photo at left) to angry and sullen, when they drink. These mood swings create a "Jekyll-and-Hyde" personality that can cause family problems.

Even "happy" drinkers can become alcoholics if and when they develop a dependency on alcohol in order to function. The reasons for their drinking and the effect it can have on others may be just as deep and dark as those of the "mean drunk."

Ted, for example, remembers his father as a surly man, gruff and difficult to get along with, until after he'd had a drink. Then he became much more pleasant and easygoing, fun to be around. He never got drunk, he just seemed unable to relate to people without alcohol. Ted considers his father to be an alcoholic, however, because he is incapable of functioning without drinking. Their relationship is strained because Ted believes it is the alcohol, and not his father, that makes their relationship tolerable. Ted should know, having been "a real heavy drug and alcohol abuser" himself for many years.

Linda recalls her former father-in-law as a man who, when he drank, got "silly and sloppy, but always managed to find his way home." His son, Steve—her husband—however, was affected very differently by alcohol. "When he drank you never knew what would happen, or where he'd wind up. It was very unpredictable. It affected him very badly." Despite their different reactions to alcohol, Linda considers both men to be alcoholics. "There was always a party going on at my father-in-law's house. And the parties revolved around getting drunk. It wasn't just drinking occasionally like a normal home. It was constant, never-ending drinking. My father-in-law couldn't function without a drink in his belly and another in his hand." She also believes her husband's alcoholism—and his eventual suicide—were directly related to the abusive drinking that went on in the family.

"When Steven tried to stop drinking, his father called him a wimp and a failure. He told Steven a 'real man' could handle his liquor. He taunted him constantly and made his life miserable. He made him feel as if he really was a failure."

Some researchers estimate that every alcoholic negatively affects the lives of at least five other people. John Bradshaw, a family therapist and a recovering alcoholic himself, tells a story that demonstrates the subtle destructiveness of the "happy drunk." It is a story about a little child whose mother, when sober, yells at him for being such a brat. After she's had a drink, however, she kisses him and apologizes. After a couple more drinks, she's telling him what a wonderful child he is and about how she's going to buy him a beautiful bicycle. Come morning, when she's sober again, the bicycle is long forgotten, and the child is once again "a little brat." At least until that night, when she's had a couple more drinks.... Is the woman an alcoholic? It would certainly seem so. What's more, her drinking is having a serious and damaging effect on her child. The child "knows" it is just the alcohol that makes him look good in Mommy's eyes. This reinforces the child's fears that deep down, he really is a brat or a bad child.

DRINKING REALLY DOES MAKE YOU STUPID

In each of the cases covered in this chapter we have seen how people often abuse alcohol as a means of coping with feelings of social or psychological inadequacy. This is a good introduction to what Dr. Marc Kern, director of Addiction Alternatives (a drug and alcohol rehabilitation program), calls a pattern of "un-learning."

"Drinking really does make you stupid. It un-teaches you things. Not [subjects like] math or science or English, but other skills that are often as important—if not more so. For example, if you are fair, but not great, at being social, if you are the kind of person who goes to a dance and stands off in the corner but never gets up the nerve to ask a girl to dance, you would, if you persisted in going to more dances, eventually learn how to be a more social person. You'd develop the poise and confidence you needed to not only ask someone to dance but to actually dance with them, and then talk to them afterwards, let them know you liked them, and find out that they liked you, too. But if instead you found the short-cut I call 'the elixir,' if you discovered that by drinking you automatically became more social, then you'd think, 'I don't have to learn how to be confident with girls. I don't have to learn how to dance.'

"What drinking does in this situation is it un-learns all your other coping skills. It literally takes their place. And the reason so many people find it so hard to give up the elixir, to give up the alcohol or the drugs or both, is because after a while the coping skill they originally used it for completely evaporates. And they're stuck—they have to return to the drugs and the alcohol to do anything.

"Think about the legs on a chair. When there are four legs, then a chair is stable. When you as a person have lots of different ways of making yourself feel good, of coping with your problems, then you're stable, too. But over the course of many years, people give up these ways of coping with life because alcohol works so efficiently and effectively and on command. Pretty soon what was a stable system turns into an unstable one, where you're standing on one leg and don't know how to do anything without the 'crutch' of alcohol. I know people who knew more at one day old than they do at age 50. Even a day-old baby knows how to fall asleep, but some alcoholics become so dependent upon alcohol to sedate them into sleep, that without it, they can't sleep at all. Imagine being so stupid that you've forgotten how to fall asleep."

3

CROSSING THE LINE

*Wine makes a man better pleased with himself; I do not say
that it makes him more pleasing to others.*
—Samuel Johnson

"I started drinking when I was 11," says Tim. "My first drink was magic. I didn't kind of slowly trend towards alcoholism, I came out of the gate on a rampage. Ever since the first drink I had, I realized alcohol was my best friend. It was my medicine. I was willing to do anything I had to do to preserve my right to keep drinking."

There is always an exception to every rule, and this is especially true when it comes to the "rules" about alcoholism. Even though Tim's addiction to alcohol began differently from most, it very quickly fell into a typical alcoholic pattern. Luckily, Tim was able to get help before he had done too much serious harm to either himself or those around him.

"My parents are both nonalcoholics. I had a wonderful childhood and family life. I guess I'd have to describe myself as the dysfunctional part of a very functional family.

"I was almost strictly a beer alcoholic. I did experiment with drugs, but alcohol was my medicinal thing, so that even when I wasn't doing drugs I was drinking. I was able to maintain fairly well for a few years. I was able to go to school and eventually graduate from high school, all while drinking every day. And I did drink every day. I was one of those kinds of drinkers. By the time I was 17 or 18 I was

When does drinking for pleasure turn into a drinking problem? The line between problem drinking and alcoholism is a slim one.

drinking around the clock, but still managing pretty well. I lied to my family, made them think I was just going through a phase, that I was still in control of the thing, but then everything just suddenly went to hell.

"My downfall was drinking and driving. By the time I was 18 I'd had six DUIs, five of them felony counts. Luckily I never killed anyone, but I did hurt this one woman.

"I was just going out to the corner store to get some more beer and made a left turn in front of her. Nothing major, but she was pretty banged up and broke a finger in the process. When the police arrived I ran. That was my thing, to panic and run and hope no one would catch me, but they always did. So there was this car chase afterwards, and I wound up with all these guns in my face. But that night was the last night I ever drank.

"I was ready to quit, I guess. No, I *know* I was ready. I was done. I'd had enough. I was in jail, I was at a point where I said to myself, 'Do you want to live or die?' I knew if I kept drinking I'd die. I had to quit. My tolerance was gone. I couldn't predict with any certainty what would happen after that first drink. There was a time when I could drink a 12-pack of beer and carry on a conversation as if nothing were wrong—except that I wouldn't remember any of it in the morning. Then, after a while, I'd have just two drinks and be completely drunk."

WHEN DRINKING BECOMES A PROBLEM

Jennifer and Karen both drank as a way to cope with the pain they felt from being abused by their parents. Jeffrey drank as a way to escape the pressure he felt from his father to excel at school and in sports. Tony didn't start drinking until he went to college. "College was a lot harder than I thought it would be, and I was having a hard time keeping up," he remembers. "Mostly it was because, back in high school, I was a star athlete. But at college I was just a nobody. I didn't even make the team. It kind of threw me. Everything was different than I had expected. I wasn't the center of attention any more. But when I drank, people paid attention, because I would do these really crazy—no, really stupid—things. It was the only way I could be a part of the 'in' crowd." By his junior year, Tony had flunked out of school. A few months later he checked into an alcohol rehabilitation center.

Why people drink may have as much to do with whether or not they develop a drinking problem as how much they drink. The line between "acceptable" and "unacceptable" drinking, however, is often blurred. What may be acceptable in one situation or with one group might be completely unacceptable in another.

In a society that seems to tolerate occasional alcohol abuse, knowing where to draw the line can be very confusing. Literally "crossing the line" while driving—that is, being so impaired that you are unable to control your car's path on the road—is clearly unacceptable under any conditions.

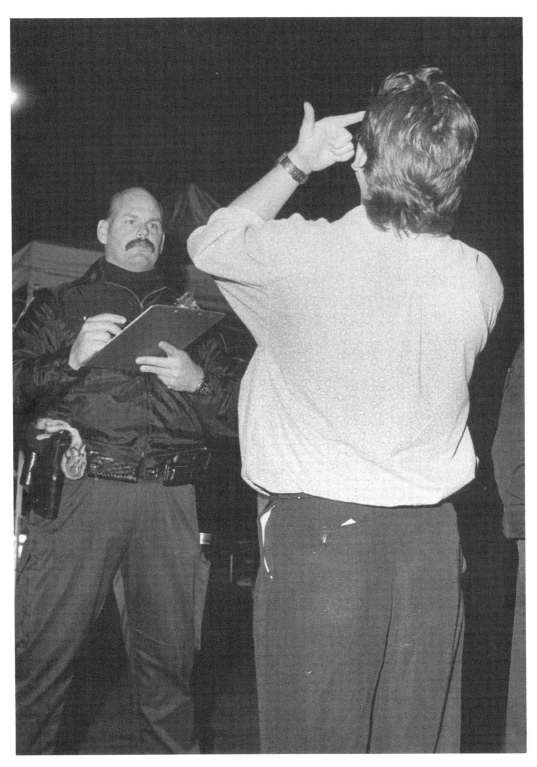

Drunk drivers have become such a problem that "sobriety checkpoints" are a common sight along our highways.

By definition, alcohol "use" is use in moderation. Alcohol "abuse" is anything in excess of moderation. Getting drunk, therefore, is alcohol abuse. Abuse of any drug can be extremely dangerous. While most people would agree that getting drunk is not the same thing as being an alcoholic, abusing alcohol can have serious physical and psychological consequences. Even moderate drinking can be damaging. If alcohol is playing even a small role in any other problems a person is having, then that person has a problem with alcohol as well.

There is no magic formula for determining how many drinks it takes to make someone into an alcoholic. Everyone has a different physical make-up. Experts may disagree whether alcoholism is a genetic, chemical, psychological or behavioral problem, but one thing is clear: many people behave very badly under the influence of alcohol. They either act out in ways that are unacceptable or, alternatively, become so withdrawn and passive that they are unable to function on a daily basis.

Often a person will use alcohol as a way of hiding problems. Since alcohol lowers inhibitions, a person who has problems with self-confidence, for example, will often feel more confident when drinking. Because alcohol also depresses the part of the brain responsible for self-consciousness and good judgment, a drinker is more likely to engage in high-risk behaviors such as unprotected sex or driving while intoxicated.

A young man might feel more confident sexually when he drinks. He may want his girlfriend to drink with him so that she will be a more willing sexual partner or be less critical of his sexual performance. A young woman may be debating with herself about whether or not to have sex. By getting drunk, however, and giving up her ability to make good judgments, she can have sex and say it "just happened." In this case, "just happens" probably means unsafe sex. Blaming alcohol is not an excuse, it's a sign of problem drinking.

Problem drinking is nothing new. It is as old as drinking itself. The Old Testament contains a story about Noah, who became drunk and stripped off his clothes, embarrassing his sons. Even an ancient Egyptian book of etiquette warns about the consequences of drunken behavior.

By lowering or "depressing" a person's inhibitions, alcohol encourages behavior that might not otherwise be considered acceptable. Many problem drinkers become extremely boisterous. They are loud and frequently obnoxious. Their every emotion is heightened and magnified. Feelings and resentments previously kept hidden bubble to the surface.

Problem drinkers are often irresponsible and unreliable. They lose their sense of balance and yet think they are completely in control. They may act upon their sexual or physical impulses without thinking through all the consequences of their actions. They are definitely not all fun and laughs.

What is the difference between a person who has a drinking problem and someone who is an alcoholic? According to John Baker of the National

Council on Alcoholism and Drug Dependency (NCADD), "a person who has a drinking problem is someone who abuses alcohol, eventually realizes that they abuse alcohol, and decides not to abuse alcohol anymore." An alcoholic, according to Mr. Baker, is someone "who is obsessed with alcohol. Even though they may know they have a problem, they still can't stop drinking. They are powerless over that first drink. After it, there is no telling when they will stop or what they will do."

Baker agrees with the NCADD position that alcoholism is a disease. "It has all the components of a disease. It is a progressive condition, meaning it gets worse over time. It is beyond the control of the person who is afflicted. Left untreated, it can eventually lead to death."

Those experts who don't believe that alcoholism is a disease do agree that it is an addiction, one that can and often does lead to severe physical and mental damage or death. Ironically, drinking is rarely recognized as a problem until it begins to create problems for other people—that is, at the point where the drinker's behavior is no longer acceptable to those around him or her. By that time, most experts agree, the alcoholic's condition is already well advanced and difficult to treat.

A person does not just wake up one morning an alcoholic. As a progressive condition, alcoholism develops over time. Clark Vaughn, a recovering alcoholic who wrote a book about his experiences, refers to alcoholism as "the slippery slide." Over time a person can "slip" from being a social drinker to being a problem drinker to being an alcoholic without even realizing it. By the time they do, or by the time those around them finally catch on, it is nearly too late. The road back will be extremely difficult.

HOW MUCH IS TOO MUCH?

While one or two drinks is usually a safe amount for a normal-sized adult, some people are "one drink drunks." They have a very low tolerance for alcohol. They aren't able to maintain control even after drinking only a very small amount of alcohol. Other people seem to have a "hollow leg"—they can drink massive quantities of alcohol without appearing to get drunk. Is there any way to establish a guideline to help someone decide when he or she has had too much?

Alcohol can't affect a person's behavior or performance until it reaches the bloodstream. Measuring the amount of alcohol in the bloodstream will indicate how impaired a person's psychomotor skills have become; that is, how much control they have over both their behavior ("psycho") and their physical performance ("motor").

A blood alcohol content (BAC) test is considered to be the best way of determining when a person had too much to drink. For example, when a person is arrested for driving under the influence, a BAC test can often be used in court as evidence of their physical impairment. Not everyone agrees, however, what level of alcohol in the blood makes a person unable to safely operate a motor vehicle. In most states, a BAC of 0.10 percent is considered legally impaired; in a few states, however, a level of 0.08 percent is sufficient. In Sweden, a level of only 0.05 percent is the accepted limit. A level of 0.4 percent alcohol is enough to cause coma or even death in some people.

BLOOD ALCOHOL CONCENTRATION (BAC)

Ideal Body Weight (lbs.)	Males - Number of Drinks							
	1	2	3	4	5	6	7	8
100	.043	.087	.130	.174	.217	.261	.304	.348
125	.034	.069	.103	.139	.173	.209	.242	.278
150	.029	.058	.087	.116	.145	.174	.203	.232
175	.025	.050	.075	.100	.125	.150	.175	.200
200	.022	.043	.065	.087	.108	.130	.152	.174
225	.019	.039	.058	.078	.097	.117	.136	.156
250	.017	.035	.052	.070	.087	.105	.122	.139

Ideal Body Weight (lbs.)	Females - Number of Drinks							
	1	2	3	4	5	6	7	8
100	.050	.101	.152	.203	.253	.304	.355	.406
125	.040	.080	.120	.162	.202	.244	.282	.324
150	.034	.068	.101	.135	.169	.203	.237	.271
175	.029	.058	.087	.117	.146	.175	.204	.233
200	.026	.050	.076	.101	.126	.152	.177	.203
225	.022	.045	.068	.091	.113	.136	.159	.182
250	.020	.041	.061	.082	.101	.122	.142	.162

Source: The Encyclopedia of Alcoholism, O'Brien and Chafetz (Facts On File, 1982)

While a BAC test isn't always readily available, the rate at which alcohol enters the bloodstream is predictable enough that a person's BAC can be reasonably estimated by using the chart above. This chart provides a realistic guideline as to how much alcohol a person can safely drink based on their size. Note that time plays a significant factor as well. Two drinks spread out over two hours have a different effect than two drinks per hour. Because men as a rule tend to have more muscle per pound of body weight than women, the rate at which alcohol enters the bloodstream is different for men and women. A level of 0.10 percent is considered the legal limit in most states. According to this chart, an average adult—a man or woman weighing between 125 and 175 pounds—could drink one or two drinks per day without getting drunk.

Body weight and fitness have a lot to do with how much and how quickly alcohol enters the bloodstream and affects a person.

A person's size, fitness, diet, and experience with alcohol all play a role in determining his or her reaction. While a full stomach won't keep someone from getting drunk, it will slow down the rate at which alcohol enters the bloodstream. Large people have more blood than small people, so the concentration of alcohol in the blood builds up more slowly in large people. A person who is in good shape has more muscle mass and, as a result, more blood circulates throughout his system than that of a similar person who is not in good shape. People who are overweight, however, will get drunk faster than people of the same height who are thinner. This is because the more slender person has more muscle mass and more blood volume than the fatter person.

Drinking experience can also affect tolerance, but only outwardly. Many drinkers discover that as they get older, it takes more alcohol to produce the same feelings of intoxication they felt when they were younger and less experienced.

This does not mean the rate at which alcohol enters the bloodstream has changed; only the perception of the alcohol's effects (and the body's ability to adjust to its effects) has changed. A blood alcohol content test will still reveal whether their motor skills are sufficiently impaired for them to be considered legally "drunk."

Most people learn how to drink by watching their parents. When mom or dad have a drink or two (or more) at the end of the day and stay sober, the children assume alcohol will affect them the same way. This won't be the case. After only two drinks in one hour, a 100-pound girl would have a BAC of 0.101 percent, enough to be considered legally drunk in all 50 states. Her father would have a BAC of only 0.50 percent and not be considered drunk in any state.

WHAT'S SO MAGICAL ABOUT TURNING 21?

Nothing special or magical happens when a person turns 21, and yet the legal drinking age in the United States is 21 years old. It is no secret, however, that people under age 21 do drink. By most estimates, nine out of ten high school seniors have tried alcohol; three or four will have been drunk within the past week; and at least one will eventually become—or already is—an alcoholic. So why does the United States insist that people be 21 before they are legally allowed to drink? The answer is the large number of alcohol-related automobile and other accidents and deaths involving teens.

For a brief period of time during the 1970s, 18-year-olds were allowed to legally drink alcohol in some states. Other states set their own legal age between 18 and 21. The number of fatal alcohol-related accidents shot up when the drinking age was lowered to 18, and later the age limit was again raised to 21 in all 50 states. Since then, the number of fatal accidents has once again declined.

Today, drivers under the age of 21 are still involved in more fatal accidents involving alcohol than any other age group. It is interesting to note that drivers between the ages of 16 and 19 who are involved in fatal accidents have much lower BAC concentrations than any other group, reinforcing the fact that alcohol affects different people in different ways.

Why do teens have so many more alcohol-related car accidents than adults? Perhaps it is because both driving and drinking are such new experiences for teens that they have less of an ability to adapt when confronted with an unfamiliar situation. Learning to drive is hard enough by itself. A new driver has to get used to the way a car handles, has to learn how much time and space are needed to make a turn in front of another car, and has to judge the distance required to make a safe stop. Even a small amount of alcohol will dramatically affect an individual's perception of time, speed, and distance.

Denial may also play a significant role in the number of alcohol-related accidents caused by teenagers. Young people often feel invincible. They believe bad things happen to other people, not to them. The sedative effect of alcohol enhances these feelings, and encourages a drinker to take chances he or she might otherwise consider risky.

Driving under the influence and not having an accident, however, seems to "prove" just the opposite to the teen drinker. It means he or she can "handle" liquor. Jennifer, Karen, Jeffrey, and Jason all recall episodes where they drank and drove as teens and did not have an accident. They believed nothing would ever happen to them. Karen, who lost a sister in a drunk-driving accident, still insisted that "it will never happen to me." She and the other teens were all wrong. Jennifer, Jason, and Jeffrey each had accidents where their drinking was a factor. Jeffrey reports having several accidents and, while he insists he wasn't "totally drunk," he does think that "drinking definitely had something to do with it." Even so, he continued drinking and was eventually arrested for driving under the influence. For Jennifer, her accident was the turning point that made her decide to get help.

Drinking alcohol is a deadly killer when combined with driving a car. People who ignore this mixture are not only endangering themselves, but also others.

Experts used to believe that teenagers couldn't become alcoholics, but experience has shown that age doesn't matter. Many problem drinkers started abusing alcohol before they were age 12.

CAN A TEENAGER BE AN ALCOHOLIC?

Until recently, people believed that it was impossible for teenagers to become alcoholics. They might drink, and they might have problems as a result of drinking, but because alcoholism takes time to develop, there wasn't enough time during the "teen" years for someone to become a full-blown alcoholic. Today, doctors and treatment centers around the country are seeing more young people who are addicted to alcohol. Most have not yet developed physical symptoms associated with chronic alcohol abuse like liver and brain damage, but they can't quit drinking without help. Once having quit, they can't go back to drinking without picking up right where they left off and slipping back into their old habits.

Studies have shown that the earlier someone begins drinking, the more likely they are to develop a drinking problem later in life. People who don't drink until after they are 25 rarely become alcoholics. People who haven't had a drinking problem or become alcoholics by the time they are 45 are unlikely to ever do so. Among the recovering alcoholics interviewed for this book, most had started drinking between the ages of eight and 12; all were heavy drinkers by the time they were 13; and all were admitted alcoholics by the time they were in their mid-20s. In retrospect, each admits that they had drinking problems as children, and were indeed alcoholics as teenagers.

Age, however, isn't always a determining factor. People who wait until their late teens or early 20s to start drinking can still become alcoholics.

4

PATTERNS OF ABUSE

For my lungs and for my liver I do definetly fear, I like to smoke on cigarettes and drink the wine and beer.
—Loudon Wainwright III

Like many alcoholics, John's father was addicted to a number of drugs in addition to alcohol. "He had a pill to wake up in the morning, a pill to go to sleep at night, pills for pain, pills to make him happy, pills to pick him up when he was down, pills to bring him down when he was too up," John recalls. "And he'd wash them all down with a big glass of vodka."

Jeffrey remembers not realizing he had a problem with alcohol "until I did something about my cocaine problem." Karen, too, says that it was only when she admitted she had a problem with cocaine that she realized she had a problem with alcohol, too.

Jennifer took other drugs along with alcohol to help smooth out the "bumpy" parts of being drunk. "I hated getting sick and throwing up, all the dizziness, so I took drugs to get rid of that," she recalls. After running away from the scene of an auto accident while drunk, she finally admitted to her mother that she had a problem with alcohol, and agreed to go for treatment. She stopped drinking, but continued using marijuana and cocaine. Before too long she was using alcohol again, this time to help smooth out the "bumpy" parts of being high. A second try at getting sober worked, but only—she believes—because she faced the fact that she has an addictive personality. "It's just the kind of person I am. Total abstinence is the only thing that works for me."

Many people can't make it through a single day without drinking. This is just one sign of an addictive personality.

Do some people stand a better chance of becoming addicted to alcohol than others because of the "type of person" they are? Not everyone who becomes an alcoholic has an addictive personality, but many doctors and researchers believe there are certain personality types and behavior patterns that indicate someone may have an addictive personality. Addiction is a factor in many aspects of their lives, not just their drinking.

Jeffrey's experiences back this up. "I find it in many areas of my life: sex, money, school, work, people. I never can get enough. I always want more, more, more. Like with money, I'd go out and buy a lot of stuff I didn't need, just to buy it. I was a workaholic. I'd take my work home with me, let it affect my personal life. I'd use people for sex, just because. I was always trying to manipulate and control situations, making sure I got my way. The addictive thought pattern was definitely there, even as a child. And with it came feelings of isolation, of being alone. I really felt that as a kid. I grew up in a family with eight kids and it seemed like I never had enough attention. I always had to be with kids who were 'happening' so I could get attention, too. It's all part of addiction."

A number of recovering alcoholics find that while they can give up drinking, they can't give up their coffee or their cigarettes. Coffee and cigarette breaks are a regular and important part of most Alcoholics Anonymous (AA) meetings. Karen, a member of AA, admits to being a chain smoker in the same way that she was once a compulsive drinker: "I can't get through the day without them," she says, exhaling a thick cloud of smoke. In a way, she has traded one addiction for another.

Cigarettes and coffee both contain drugs that, like alcohol, are known to cause addiction. Cigarettes contain nicotine, a botanical pesticide (one that occurs naturally in plants) that first stimulates and then depresses the brain. Coffee contains a stimulant called caffeine. Addiction to caffeine and nicotine has been known to cause certain behavioral problems including irritability and an inability to focus or concentrate, especially during withdrawal. Because these symptoms are relatively mild compared to those produced by alcohol addiction, however, most people don't consider them to be as serious as other health risks associated with too much caffeine or nicotine such as lung cancer and heart disease.

What exactly is an addictive personality? Are there traits that might make someone prone to developing an addiction? If so, are they psychological or physical?

Addiction is characterized by obsession and compulsion. An obsession is an unnatural or excessive preoccupation with something. Compulsion is the uncontrollable desire to do something, even if one knows that it is harmful or dangerous. John Baker of the National Council on Alcoholism and Drug Dependency (NCADD) believes that a person can have these traits—and thus be an alcoholic—even before they've had their first drink. "Feelings of isolation,

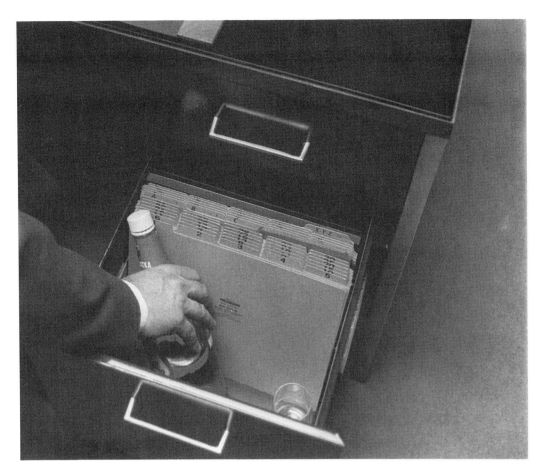

Sneaking a drink at home or at work is another sign of addiction to alcohol. The inability to function in everyday situations without alcohol should be a warning to get help.

low self-esteem, and compulsive thought patterns—never being able to get enough, always wanting more—when someone puts alcohol into a system operating with these factors, alcoholism is practically a given." It may not happen right away, but over time the use of alcohol will escalate into abuse and eventually become addiction.

The addictive personality is often someone who feels deprived of love or attention as a child, who feels he or she is different from others, but still wants to be a part of the crowd. This person is someone who has low self-esteem, yet still has that craving to be special, to get attention, to be loved.

Robert, a recovering alcoholic, believes that all alcoholics suffer from "overwhelming terror, bewilderment and despair, intense feelings of inadequacy. We don't feel as if we fit in anywhere, although we try and pretend we do. And alcohol helps. It helps erase all those bad feelings, makes us believe we really are okay, we really do fit in."

Karen remembers feeling terribly unloved as a child. Her mother abused her both physically and verbally, and she remembers with some bitterness that while "there was always enough money to buy a new car, somehow there wasn't enough money to buy food for the kids."

Jennifer, too, recalls feeling unwanted and unloved. She also remembers that her mother, who is also an alcoholic, felt much the same way. "My mom was very lonely, busy trying to make ends meet. My Dad left us for another woman and it was hard. She didn't have any friends, and she drank a lot to cope. She worked really hard and when she got home she didn't want to play with my brother or me. She just wanted to drink. She used to drink all night until she passed out. I just thought she'd fallen asleep. It made me angry that things were the way they were, so I started drinking, too."

IS ALCOHOLISM HEREDITARY?

The fact that Jennifer's mother also is an alcoholic raises another important question: How much of a person's alcoholism can be attributed to their heredity, their "genetic make-up," and how much to the environment in which he or she was raised?

The debate over nature (heredity) versus nurture (environment) has raged for decades. While the question of whether or not alcoholism is inherited may never be resolved, there is clear and compelling evidence that it does tend to run in families. "Without exception," says Washington University researcher Dr. Donald Goodwin, in his book *Is Alcoholism Hereditary?*" every family study of alcoholism has shown much higher rates of alcoholism among the relatives of alcoholics than occur in the general population. The strongest predictor of future alcoholism...is a family history of alcoholism."

There are those who insist that this theory proves there is a biological connection between parents who are alcoholics and their children who later become alcoholics. Others believe that the connection is simply the result of the way these children were raised. They learned how to be alcoholics from watching their parents.

In fact, no gene that causes alcoholism has ever been identified. Scientists tend to believe, however, that there may be a genetic tendency toward developing alcoholism in some people. They point out that there is no gene for diabetes or heart disease, and yet these diseases also tend to run in families.

It cannot be denied that alcoholism is also—at least to some degree— a learned behavior. While many children recoil in horror from watching their parents abuse alcohol and vow never to drink, others grow up believing their parent's alcoholism is normal and acceptable, and that one is supposed to abuse alcohol. The parent, by example, actually "teaches" the child to abuse alcohol.

Jordan believes he was taught to be an alcoholic. "I drank the way I did because I was taught no other social behavior. I was not taught that you could go out and play softball and have a good time without a cold beer. No one ever taught me that you could have a celebration that did not contain alcohol. I was taught that any time there was a celebration—an aunt's birthday, a wedding, the birth of a cousin—it was time to bring out the booze. Any time there were more than three people in the room at a given time was reason enough for a party. I can't think of a single exception, even my granddad's funeral. They were slamming down drinks before his casket was even wheeled down the aisle."

THE CHILDREN OF ALCOHOLICS

Children of alcoholics come from dysfunctional families. The examples set for them by their parents are disturbing and confusing. When Mom drinks too much and passes out on the sofa, she becomes an absent parent. She can't be there to give her children a hug when they need one, or praise them for the good job they did at school. On the other hand, when she isn't drinking, she may be the perfect mom. Every time Dad flies into a drunken rage, he, too, becomes incapable of being a good parent.

Because the children of alcoholics never know what to expect from their parents, their lives are in constant turmoil. They often feel as if they are to blame for their parent's drinking, and they frequently have terrible opinions of themselves. They aren't able to express their feelings well, or even acknowledge that they have feelings. Very often they find it difficult to trust others. These children also develop many of the traits of an addictive personality as they mature. They try to make up for their lost childhood and feelings of anger and frustration.

Like many children of alcoholics, Jordan exhibited signs of an addictive personality as he grew up. No matter how much he had, it wasn't enough. He wanted and needed to be the center of attention. No matter what he did, it wasn't good enough."The way I looked at it was this," he explains. "I was having a hard time balancing life in general. I was going down a real bad road. On the outside everything was great; on the inside everything was falling apart. The shell was perfect—I had the perfect car, the perfect job, but on the weekends I was getting plowed. It got to be a problem with work because Tuesday I'd finally come out of the fog and my boss would say, 'On Monday, did you do this and this and this?' and I'd say, 'Oh, no. That slipped my mind.'"

Jordan also believes that his alcoholism is partly hereditary. His grandfather was an alcoholic, both his parents are alcoholics, and most of his brothers and sisters are alcoholics. Dr. Goodwin's research led him to reach the same conclusion about people like Jordan. "The evidence that alcoholism involves a biological vulnerability is just as strong, or perhaps stronger, than the evidence that hypertension or adult onset diabetes involves a biological vulnerability," he says.

Recovering alcoholics, according to almost all the experts, can never touch alcohol again as long as they live—not even one drink at a party. Their addiction is too strong.

The case of Alice is a good example of just how tightly interwoven the environmental and hereditary factors of alcoholism are. Alice was raised in a home where drinking was forbidden. She doesn't remember ever seeing her father drink, but learned many years later that he was an alcoholic. He would drink heavily for a couple of years and then stop completely, as he did when he married Alice's mother, whose religion prohibited drinking. When the marriage fell apart, he went right back to drinking.

Alice hated the rules her parents made for her. She vowed she was going to be completely different from them. When she was 17, she started drinking and partying heavily in defiance of her strict upbringing. She would often do outrageous things when drunk, like taking off her clothes and getting into the bathtub at someone else's house. While still a teenager, she became pregnant. Unmarried, she was forced to give her child up for adoption. Continuing to drink heavily, she finally married a man from another country whose religion prohibited drinking. Immediately she gave up liquor, and didn't start drinking again until after she and her husband were divorced. In her effort to be completely different from her father, Alice became exactly like him.

Years later, after she joined AA and stopped drinking, Alice was reunited with the daughter she had given up for adoption. As it turned out, her daughter was an alcoholic, too.

Can someone who has an addictive personality ever drink safely? Most experts, including those who believe that at least some problem drinkers are able to learn how to drink responsibly, agree that total abstinence is the only cure for people who have addictive personalities and have developed an alcohol addiction. "In all my experience," says John Baker of NCADD, "I have never seen anyone who has an addictive personality drink successfully."

With the exception of Jordan, every recovering alcoholic interviewed for this book agreed that it would be impossible for them to ever drink socially again. Even Jordan admits that he may never drink again. "I prefer to say I don't drink because I choose not to," he explains. "When someone asks, 'Are you an AA member?' I say no, because I'm not. I think I practice the AA formula on my own, but AA isn't for me. If I decide at some point to have a glass of wine with dinner or a beer with friends, well then maybe I will. But for now, I choose not to drink at all."

THE POWER OF DENIAL

According to Baker, denial is "the number one symptom of addiction." Alcoholics refuse to admit that they have a problem until after it is way out of control. Deep down Karen knew she had a problem with drinking when she was just 14, but whenever a teacher or counselor would say something to her about her drinking, she would deny she had a problem. "I can quit any time I want," she'd say. But to her closest friend she once confided that she was worried about her drinking. She also wrote a poem about how "I used to control the bottle, but now the bottle controls me." It wasn't until she was in her early 20s—almost ten years later—that she finally decided she needed to get help.

Jeffrey recalls that when his parents first talked to him about his drug and alcohol use, he flatly denied he had a problem. "I enjoyed drinking and doing drugs. But the more they talked to me about there being a different way, the more those old voices started coming back to me. When you're drinking or doing drugs, there's a part of you that knows, deep down, that this is wrong, that you're hurting yourself, that there could be another, better way of life, but you never seem to be able to break away from that." Eventually, Jeffrey's mom convinced him to seek help. But by that time Jeffrey's alcohol and drug use had already caused him irreversible brain damage—damage of which he wasn't aware.

Denial can creep back into a person's life when they aren't looking. "When I told my mom I thought I had a drinking problem, she told me maybe I should go to a meeting," remembers Jennifer. "As soon as she said that, I remember thinking, I'm not that bad, really. I don't have that kind of a problem. But I did." In fact, it took Jennifer two tries to finally kick her addiction.

Just how deep does denial run? One therapist, when told of Jordan's belief that he might someday be able to drink again, claimed that Jordan is still in denial. "He doesn't want to admit to himself yet just how serious his problem is. He still wants to leave the door open to going back and drinking again."

Jordan still has a problem with being called an alcoholic. "The minute someone says, 'You're an alcoholic,' it's a stigma to me. It downgrades the person." Jordan does admit, however, that denial played a significant role in his drinking. "I was in flat denial up until age 26," he says. "I recognized I had a problem when I was 16. I knew I was using alcohol as an excuse to get away with doing things I couldn't do otherwise. The excuse was always, 'Hey, I didn't mean it, I was just drunk.' And I guess deep down I knew it was wrong. But it took me ten long years to finally really admit it.

"I went to see a counselor and he said if I didn't think I had a problem with alcohol I should try giving it up for a week. I said, 'No problem.' So I did. I gave it up for a week. Then two weeks. Then three. It got to be a game. It was a real bitch to quit. In the beginning every day was a struggle. But the minute I figured out I could turn the behavior around and say, 'This isn't going to control me,' I could lick it. I tried to minimize alcohol's role in my life by removing myself from anything that would remind me of drinking, including my family. I stopped hanging out with friends who drank. I stopped going to bars. It's all still real new for me, but I'm starting to feel like I'm in control now."

A constant need to drink to the point of drunkenness or unconsciousness is a clear signal that someone has an alcohol problem.

OTHER WARNING SIGNS

Because the line between problem drinking and alcoholism is so fuzzy, most alcoholics can't recall just when it was they became an addict. Most do recall a point at which they realized things had somehow changed. Jennifer remembers how "it got to the point where I just always wanted to be drunk. I didn't enjoy doing anything unless I was under the influence. I can remember being very young and going to the park to watch the sun set and thinking it was really neat, but then it got so I wouldn't want to go to the park unless we were stoned or drinking beer. I stopped wanting to do regular enjoyable things. I didn't want to go to parties if there wasn't going to be alcohol there. I stopped hanging around people who didn't drink as much as I did. I'd do things, talk to people, and not remember what I did. I lied all the time, broke the law. I felt bad about it, but I kept doing it anyway. My word meant nothing. But I couldn't stop."

Alcoholics sometimes suffer from blackouts, after which they can remember nothing that happened while they were drunk.

In addition to revealing certain traits of an addictive personality, Jennifer's story also shows how alcohol can "unteach" important social skills. Over time, Jennifer lost the ability to enjoy even simple things like watching a sunset or going to a party.

How can you tell if you or someone you know have a drinking problem? There are a number of warning signs that will help you decide.

First, there's drunkenness. Getting drunk is in and of itself a form of alcohol abuse. It is also a sign that a drinking problem may be or is already developing. The more frequently a person gets drunk, the more likely he or she is to develop a drinking problem.

Sneaking drinks is often the only way teenagers are able to drink, since they are forbidden by law from doing so otherwise. Regardless of whether a person is 14 or 40, hidden drinking is a strong indicator of a drinking problem. It implies feelings of guilt, and at least a subconscious recognition that the amount of drinking that is going on is excessive. It is impossible to use alcohol socially when one is drinking alone. Hidden drinking, therefore, is a warning sign.

People who are able to drink a lot are at an increased risk of drinking too much. While *being able to "hold one's liquor"* is often looked upon as a good thing, it can lead to both problem and addictive drinking. Watch for this type of high tolerence of alcohol.

Drinkers search out other drinkers. People like to be around people who are like them. Abusive drinkers find that the feelings of guilt they have from drinking too much are easier to deal with if everyone around them also drinks too much. So observe carefully if the person suspected of alcoholism changes friends.

Alcoholics frequently have trouble at home, work, or school. They struggle to maintain the outward appearance of "being normal." This helps them deny their problem, and it works—for a while. Eventually the walls come crashing down around them.

Many problem drinkers eventually find themselves acting in ways they once considered completely inappropriate. They are willing to do almost anything to continue drinking, even if it means lying, cheating, or stealing. Psychologists call this behavior "acting out."

When a person blacks out or passes out, these are serious indications of an alcohol problem. A blackout isn't the same thing as "passing out." Passing out occurs when too much alcohol enters the bloodstream, and the brain is no longer able to maintain consciousness. During a blackout, the drinker never loses consciousness, but later cannot remember anything he or she has done during this period.

When a person needs "just one more drink," addiction is not far away. Wanting a drink is one thing, but "needing" a drink—any craving for alcohol—is an indication that someone is becoming a substance abuser.

Sometimes the desire to drink is so intense that the person loses control of when, where, and how much they drink. Soon, they may have an inability to function without alcohol. The person who has to have a drink to get up in the morning, who needs alcohol before facing a crowd, going to a party, taking a test, or talking to a particular person (like a family member), has a serious drinking problem and needs immediate help.

One or two of these warning signs is usually enough to indicate a serious drinking problem. All of them are evident to varying degrees in the stories told by Jeffrey, Karen, Jennifer, Robert, and Jordan. Yet it took each of them an average of ten years to admit that they had a problem. At each new warning sign they were able, like many others, to convince themselves that nothing was wrong.

Many alcoholics hide their problem by drinking only when others aren't around or by sneaking a drink early in the morning.

BREAKING THROUGH THE BARRIERS

Adolescent addiction counselor Jeffory Throgmorton knows what he's talking about when it comes to teenage alcohol addiction. He began drinking at age 14 as a way of coping with his embarrassment over being small for his age. A beer or two before a school dance gave him greater confidence, and made it easier for him to talk to girls.

Eventually that beer or two evolved into a serious addiction to alcohol and other drugs. Jeffory was 35 before he admitted to himself that he had a problem with drugs and alcohol. It took him another four years before he sought help. During these four years, Jeffory struggled by himself to break his addictions. He would quit for a short time, but before long slipped back into his old habits. On a Thanksgiving weekend when he was 43, feeling completely hopeless, Jeffory took a gun and placed it to his head. He couldn't pull the trigger. Something inside him wanted to give it one more try. Jeffory put down the gun and checked himself into Charter Hospital, a private rehabilitation facility. Three years later he became a staff member at the hospital, dedicating himself to helping young people break their addictions.

"Teens have a built-in sense of indestructibility. They simply don't believe anything bad is ever going to happen to them. I think nature provides them with that feeling to help protect them from going crazy. If a kid walked around all day worried that an airplane might drop out of the sky at any minute and crash right on top of him, he wouldn't be able to spend much time being a kid. Sure, things like that happen, but 'not to me.'

"The problem is, once they start messing around with drugs and alcohol, things really do start happening to them. But they can't see it, because of the booze and because they just don't believe it could happen to them. Only about one in 20 of the kids we see here at Charter come here because they think they have a problem. The rest are here because somebody else is making them come. That one kid who knows he or she has a problem is really special, and they'll probably be okay once they get through the program. But for the others, it's going to be a tough road. We have to spend a lot of time just making them realize how much trouble they're already in.

"We start by working on all the bad things that have happened to them while they were drinking. We make a list of 25 things. At first they can only think of a few, but we keep going at it, and soon they have their list. It usually takes about three weeks of intensive, in-patient therapy just to make them realize they have a problem."

5

If Someone Close Drinks Too Much

The family can be the key to initial recovery. If the family gets into treatment there is a 90 percent chance that the alcoholic will also enter treatment.
—National Council on Alcoholism and Drug Addiction

"I hated my father," Betsy recalls. "He'd get drunk almost every night. It wasn't like he'd do anything—I mean, he didn't beat me up or anything like that...he'd just sit there watching the TV, drinking beer until he passed out. That's all he'd ever do. He'd come home from work, be nice to me for about five minutes, then open a beer and start drinking. After a couple of beers it was like I wasn't even there any more. Actually, he was the one who wasn't there. I guess that's why I hated him so much. Because even though he was my father, he never acted like a father. In a way, it was even worse than having no father at all, because I could see him sitting there, drinking, but he was never there for me when I needed him. He loved his beer more than he loved me, and I was always the one who had to clean up the mess after he passed out. It was like I was his father, instead of the other way around."

For Kyle, the situation was completely different. "My father would come looking for me when he got drunk," he remembers. "It was like he went crazy or something....He'd be screaming about how

Ironically, it is loved ones such as children and spouses who suffer most when a parent is an alcoholic.

I'd done him wrong somehow, done something that pissed him off, and he was going to teach me a lesson. That was his big thing—how he was going to teach me a lesson. Then he'd start beating on me, whipping me with his belt, and punching me. Most of the time I just took it. I don't know why. I was scared, I guess. I was just a little kid—what could I do?

"The next morning, he'd forget all about it, like it never happened. My mom, my sister, everybody just pretended nothing had happened. I started to think I was going crazy, that it was all just my imagination, but then I'd look in the mirror and I'd see the bruises, and I knew what had happened. I knew."

Alcoholism is as prevalent as it is confusing. The chances are good that you, or someone you know, lives with an alcoholic. One in five Americans grows up in a home with an alcoholic. Because of the role alcoholism plays in family violence, child abuse, incest, and other violent crimes, children of alcoholics are often at an increased risk of becoming victims of a violent crime.

Research conducted by the National Association for Children of Alcoholics (NACoA) concluded that the children of alcoholics "often adapt to the chaos and inconsistency of an alcoholic home by developing an inability to trust, an extreme need to control, excessive sense of responsibility and denial of feelings, all of which result in low self-esteem, depression, isolation, guilt and difficulty maintaining satisfying relationships."

PARENTS WHO DRINK

Children of alcoholics are often forced into taking on responsibilities that rightly belong to the parents. In fact, the parent/child roles we normally associate with being a "family" are often reversed when one or both parents are alcoholics. In the alcoholic family, it is frequently the child who must take care of the drunk or abusive parent.

Families often organize themselves around the needs and behaviors of the alcoholic. Children of alcoholics often find themselves cleaning up after a parent when the parent is so drunk that he or she spills things or makes a mess of the house. Children of alcoholics frequently play nursemaid to the parent who is sick from drinking too much. They take on the responsibility of caring for younger siblings who can't fend for themselves. Because they are denied the opportunity to be children themselves, they often never learn how to have fun and be playful.

As John Bradshaw points out, when a parent doesn't play the role that is expected of him or her, the child will often try to fill the void by becoming a superachiever. Sometimes the child responds to discord in the family by trying to be the peacemaker, the clown who breaks the tension, or the scapegoat who takes responsibility for what is wrong. It is never the child's fault when a parent drinks too much, and yet in each of these situations the child is responding to a problem in the family as if he or she were responsible. When the problem doesn't go away—when the parent continues to drink—the child feels like a failure. There may also be "rules" the child has to follow when a parent drinks, like don't say anything to anyone else about this. Don't let anyone else know what is going on. Be careful if someone asks about your parent's drinking, as they only want to cause harm. These rules can foster anxiety and mistrust in a child, and make it more difficult for him or her to relate to others. They also contribute to what is known as a co-dependency, a situation in which one person—often a spouse or child—becomes dependent upon another person's addiction.

Being a co-dependent does not mean that you are also an addict. In a co-dependent relationship, a person with low self-esteem discovers that he feels better about himself when he "helps" the person who is addicted. Covering up for that person's addiction, taking care of him when he is sick, even bringing him the alcohol or drug that caused the problem in the first place all help the co-dependent feel better about him or herself. In fact, without the addicted person in his life, he would feel completely worthless. He depends on the other person's addiction almost as much as the addict depends on the drug. "My Daddy needs me to take care of him," is the thought that runs through many a co-dependent child's mind. "He needs me."

Children of alcoholics are at greater risk of becoming alcoholics themselves than children of nonalcoholics. In families where one parent is an alcoholic, that parent's children stand a one-in-three chance of also becoming alcoholics. In families where both parents are alcoholics, the odds are one-in-two. One-half of all children from families where both parents are alcoholics become alcoholics themselves.

John's story bears out many of these statistics. Coming from a family where one parent was an alcoholic, John and his sister never developed an alcohol dependency themselves, but their brother did. John doesn't consider himself to be a very trusting person, and recognizes his extreme need to always be in control. Even his choice of profession, that of airline pilot, reflects a constant need for total control. John has problems with self-esteem and has been married three times. Both his brother and his sister have also been married and divorced several times.

Alcoholism has been known to "skip" a generation, which means that if a grandparent is an alcoholic, the parent might not be, but the grandchild stands a good chance of becoming an alcoholic. Because the children of alcoholics so often have problems with their own self-esteem, and because they have such difficulty interacting socially with others, they frequently pass these problems on to their own children.

The effects of alcohol on children of alcoholics can begin even before a child is born. As the National Association for Children of Alcoholics points out, "medical research has shown that children born to alcoholics are at the highest risk for developing attention deficit disorders, stress-related medical problems, fetal alcohol syndrome, and other alcohol-related birth defects." Not only are these problems serious in their own right, they can and frequently do contribute to other socializing problems from which the children of alcoholics so frequently suffer.

It doesn't have to be this way. The children of alcoholics can "bounce back" and lead happy, productive, well-rounded lives—especially if they get help early. If you are the child of an alcoholic, it is very important that you realize that your parent's drinking problem is not your fault. You did not cause the problem, and you do not need to fix it in order to feel good about yourself. The only person you need to take care of is yourself.

LOOKING OUT FOR NUMBER ONE

Living with a parent with a drinking problem is an extremely difficult position for a young person. Parents, just because they are parents, are in an automatic position of authority over their children. They set the rules and call the shots. They're also bigger and stronger. It can be very scary living with someone bigger than you who has a drinking problem. There's no telling what they might do.

Children of alcoholics face tough challenges, living with a parent who is not only more powerful in size but also lacking self-control.

It is often difficult for parents and children to communicate, even when alcohol isn't a factor. When alcohol is part of the problem, the difficulties increase. Some experts recommend that a child never directly confront a parent about his or her drinking. Instead, they suggest that the child contact another adult trained in handling alcohol-related problems. This adult might be found through your school, church, a local hospital, or one of the many national and government organizations set up to deal with alcohol abuse. Let this person recommend the best steps to take.

Perhaps they will first want to discuss the problem with the parent one-on-one, but this can backfire. Often the intrusion of a "stranger" into a family's personal business will cause a parent with a problem to become upset and refuse help altogether. Remember, most alcoholics are in a state of denial. They will almost always refuse to admit that there is a problem when confronted, and especially when caught off guard.

BEFORE CONFRONTING A PARENT ABOUT DRINKING

Before confronting a parent about his or her drinking problem, it is important to get help for yourself first.

- Talk to a counselor at school, or a member of the clergy.

- Call one of the programs specifically designed to help young people whose lives are affected by alcoholism.

- Learn as much as you can about alcoholism and addiction.

- Try to attend Al-Anon or Alateen meetings in your area. Even if you decide they aren't right for you, the support and information you will receive can help.

- Request brochures and other information. The more you know, the better you'll feel and the easier it will be to break the family cycle of alcohol dependency.

Getting help for yourself from someone knowledgeable is the first and most important step. If only one parent is an alcoholic, then you might want to talk to the other parent about getting help, too. Most experts suggest that you do so only after you've gotten help for yourself. Remember that the spouse of an alcoholic is often co-dependent. Denial plays as large a role in co-dependency as it does in alcoholism itself. So a co-dependent spouse will likely deny that there even is a drinking problem.

If you do decide to try talking to your parents about their drinking, most therapists recommend that you wait until they are sober. "Trying to talk to someone about their drinking when they're drunk is never a good idea," says Dr. Kern. "But talking to them the next morning, when they're still a little hung over and may be feeling guilty about their drinking might work." He cautions, however, that it is important not to accuse the person of being bad, or belittle them for their behavior. This will only push them further into a state of denial. Instead, try speaking with them calmly and rationally about how their drinking makes you feel.

CHANGE DOESN'T COME OVERNIGHT

Remember that denial is an extremely powerful component of alcoholism. It is unrealistic to expect that you will be able to sit down with your mom or dad, explain to them that you think they have a drinking problem, and have him or her agree to quit drinking right away. An alcoholic is much more likely to refuse to accept the fact that they have a problem than someone who is not an alcoholic but occasionally abuses alcohol. It takes time to break through that barrier. In some cases, it may prove impossible. You cannot force another person to stop drinking, but you can help them to see that there are other options available. In the end, though, the final decision is theirs. Even if you can't convince your mom or dad to stop drinking, you can break the cycle of addiction simply by not becoming an alcoholic yourself. This is why it is so important that you take care of yourself first.

If you aren't able to convince a parent that he or she has a problem, but you are able to get other members of your family to agree with you, you might—as a group—want to try something called an intervention. During an intervention, the family confronts the alcoholic directly as a group. They do not attack the person for drinking or tell them that they are a bad person because they drink. Instead, they explain how they feel the person's drinking is affecting his

RECOMMENDATIONS BY THE CENTER FOR SUBSTANCE ABUSE PREVENTION

The following is a list of recommendations taken from information provided by the Center for Substance Abuse Prevention.

• Do remain calm, unemotional, and factually honest about your parents' behavior when they drink.

• Don't threaten, bribe, preach, or try to punish your parents for drinking.

• Do let them know that you have been reading and learning about alcoholism, and share with them some of the things you have learned. Help them to see that their addiction is hurting them and their family. Explain to them that because alcohol is playing a role in other problems that they have, they have a problem with alcohol.

• Don't allow yourself to cover up or make excuses for their behavior. Don't help them hide their drinking or throw their liquor out for them. Don't ride in a car with them if they have been drinking.

• Do include them in your life. Help them to see that there are lots of things you can do together that don't involve drinking.

• Don't drink with them.

• Do be patient. Alcoholism takes years to develop; recovery won't happen overnight. Accept that there will be setbacks and relapses, but don't give up.

• Don't feel guilty or responsible for their behavior.

or her life and the lives of the people around them. (At the end of this book is a list of organizations that can provide you with information about how to conduct an intervention.)

One example of an intervention was when President Gerald Ford's family conducted one in the White House for Mrs. Ford. They talked to her about what they saw happening, and encouraged her to get help for her drinking and drug problem. She did, and went on to found the Betty Ford Clinic, one the most prestigious centers in the country for helping people overcome addiction.

IF A FRIEND DRINKS TOO MUCH

"I guess I knew pretty early on that Lisa had a drinking problem," remembers Sandy about the girl who was her best friend at a foreign boarding school. "The drinking age was a lot younger [in Europe]. Every time we'd go out, Lisa would get drunk. When she got drunk, she got depressed. But I really didn't know at the time what the problem was. I didn't know that much about alcoholism, and I thought it would be embarrassing for her to talk about it.

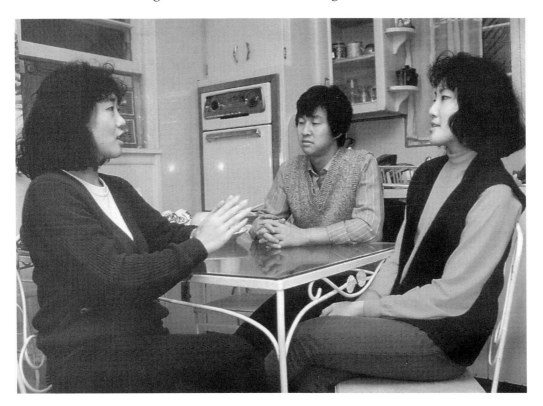

Conducting an intervention involves two or more people (usually friends or relatives) who confront a person with an alcohol problem and convince that person to get help.

"Later, after college, we lived together for awhile, and that's when things got really bad. She'd go out to a bar alone and not come home until the next day. She'd wind up sleeping with some guy she didn't even know, and then spend the night at his house but swear to me that she didn't remember....After we stopped living together I called her one time, and she was so drunk that the next day she didn't even recall talking to me. That's when I told her she had a problem. But she wouldn't talk about it, and I didn't know what to do, so that was that. We just never talked about it."

The odds are that, like Sandy, you already know someone at school who has a serious problem with alcohol. While more adults have drinking problems than teenagers, one in 15 teens will have a serious drinking problem by the time he or she graduates from high school. One in eight will develop a serious problem with alcohol as an adult. If there are 30 students in your classroom right now, at least three may become alcoholics one day. Two of them might already have—or will soon develop—a drinking problem.

Teenagers are stuck in the awkward position of no longer being children, but not quite being adults. "Childish" things are left behind or exchanged for more "adult" experiences like going out on dates, driving, or getting a job. Experimenting with alcohol has become a "normal" part of growing up in the United States, because drinking is considered to be a "normal" adult activity.

Teenagers can often take classes to learn how to drive or get a job. Learning how to drink, however, is not a part of the school curriculum. Teens learn how to drink from other teens, their families, and watching adults around them. Since many adults have drinking problems, it should come as no surprise that a large number of teenagers quickly develop their own drinking problems.

WARNING SIGNS OF A PROBLEM

If a friend of yours tells you he got drunk at a recent party, does that mean he has a problem? Not necessarily. But it could be a sign that a problem might develop later. Repeated episodes of drunkenness are definitely an indication of a drinking problem.

If someone you know ever passes out at a party from too much alcohol, he or she not only has a drinking problem, but also an immediate medical emergency as well. Passing out is a sign of a dangerously high blood alcohol content. Teens often think a person who has passed out just needs to "sleep it off," but someone who becomes unconscious while drinking may be suffering from alcohol poisoning. In fact, it could prove fatal if he or she doesn't receive immediate medical attention. You may be afraid to get help because you are worried about getting in trouble, but the unconscious person is already in serious medical trouble. Ask an adult or call for help immediately.

Teenagers who have a drinking problem often overindulge at athletic events and parties, to the point where they become ill and pass out.

A teen who frequently drinks or gets drunk has an obvious drinking problem, but there are other signs to look for as well. Use the following checklist if you believe someone you know has a drinking problem.

- *Frequent drinking.* If you know someone who drinks a lot of alcohol more than once or twice a month, even if they never get drunk, you know someone who either has or is developing a drinking problem.
- *Obsession with alcohol.* If someone you know talks about drinking a lot, or if they arrange their schedule around events where alcohol will be available, such as parties and sporting events, this is a sure sign that he or she has a drinking problem.
- *Inability to socialize without alcohol.* If you have friends who will only go to parties where alcohol is present, or if they are too self-conscious to talk to others without first having a drink, they have a drinking problem.

Many teens conceal their drinking, becoming caught up in a web of lies about their drinking problem.

- *Changes in mood or attitude.* Mood swings, losing interest in school, and hanging out with a different crowd may all be indications of a drinking or other drug-related problem.
- *Being drunk at school or missing school.* When a person's education is being affected by alcohol, it is a definite indication of a serious drinking problem and may even be a cry for help.
- *Lying about drinking.* Lying about drinking is a symptom of denial. Just as with hidden drinking, people who lie about whether or how much they drink have a drinking problem.
- *Hidden drinking.* A person who feels a need to hide the fact that he has been drinking has, by definition, a drinking problem. He is in a serious state of denial, and will have a hard time facing the fact that he needs help.
- *Drinking and driving.* Drinking and driving in any combination is an indication of a serious drinking problem. Never, under any circumstances, get in a car with someone who has been drinking.

Teenagers run an especially high risk of becoming alcoholics because of circumstances that often surround their drinking. Since drinking is illegal for those under age 21, many young people feel a need to hide their drinking. They will also lie about it when they get caught, for fear of being punished. This situation often becomes dangerous for them and others when they choose to drive under the influence. It becomes very easy for a teenager to develop a drinking problem because he or she will begin to act just like an alcoholic: drinking just to get drunk; lying about drinking to keep from getting in trouble with mom or dad; trying to hide one's drinking; and driving while drunk so no one will find out that he or she is drunk.

THE NEXT STEP

What can you do if you think a friend might have a drinking problem? There are several options. The relationship between friends is often more trusting than that between parent and child. A teenager is much more likely to listen to or be influenced by someone his or her own age, someone they respect. Also, it is much easier to stop a problem when it is caught in the early stages. A teen with a drinking problem has probably only been drinking for a short period of time—a few years at most. Adults with drinking problems have often been drinking since they were teenagers.

The best thing you can do is set a good example. Don't allow yourself to slip into the same kinds of traps your friend has fallen into. If you drink at a party, drink only in moderation. Don't get drunk, and don't ever drive or ride with anyone who has been drinking. If you aren't drinking, offer to be a

Don't let anyone drive drunk. Alcohol causes impairment of the senses, yet those under its influence think they are sharper, or say they "can handle it." They can't.

designated driver. A designated driver is a person who promises not to drink any alcoholic beverages, and provides transportation for those who do drink so they won't have to drive themselves.

Alternatively, you could be the "keymaster." The keymaster collects car keys from everyone who drove to the party, then only returns them to owners who are sober. Together with others at the party who haven't been drinking, the keymaster makes sure that everyone who is too drunk to drive gets a safe ride home.

If you're concerned about the drinking habits of a close friend, talk to him privately, and explain why you're worried. Don't criticize or try to make him feel bad. Be supportive, and offer to help in any way you can. Let him know that you still want to be friends. If this person agrees to get help, go with him to an AA or Alateen meeting. Don't be surprised, however, if your friend denies there is a problem. It isn't an easy thing to admit. Continue to read and learn more about alcoholism, then share what you learn. It is important that your friend know you'll be there for them through their recovery.

WHAT IF THEY REFUSE?

If your friend refuses to get help, or if the person isn't close enough for you to confront alone, try approaching him or her as part of a concerned group of friends—conduct an intervention as described earlier. This works to your advantage in two ways: you will probably be more comfortable than you would be talking to the person alone, and he or she will probably be more willing to admit that there's a problem if several people say there is. Many teens develop a drinking problem precisely because they don't feel as if they fit in with "the group." If "the group" comes to them and says, "Hey, we like you, and you're a part of us, but we're concerned about what you're doing to yourself," a positive response is much more likely.

6

IF YOU DRINK TOO MUCH

The first step in treatment is hope.
—George Valliant, Harvard University

If, after reading this book, you think you might have a drinking problem yourself, you are already well on the road to recovery. You've broken through that thick veil of denial. Self-awareness is the biggest hurdle, so the hardest part is already over.

On the other hand, maybe you don't believe you have a problem—at least not yet. Maybe you're just curious about what could happen if you ever do. You know that alcoholism runs in your family, and you want to make sure it doesn't happen to you. Maybe you're curious about what it's like for someone to realize they have a drinking problem. You might be thinking about someone you know, someone you're concerned about, and what they're going through. No matter what your reason, keep reading. There's something here for you.

USE, ABUSE, OR DEPENDENCE?

We've seen how easy it is to slide from use into abuse, then into dependence. We've also seen how denial can creep back in, even after someone admits to having a problem. The longer a problem has been going on, the harder it is to kick the habit. It can be done if you get help and stick with it.

How can you tell when you have a drinking problem? One way is telling yourself that you can stop anytime—but you never do. This is known as denial.

Alcohol dependence rarely happens with the first drink. More often, it takes years to develop. Some therapists believe that if a person is abusing alcohol but hasn't yet become dependent upon it, they can be "taught" how to drink more responsibly. They can learn when and how to use alcohol without abusing it. If you are a teenager who has only recently begun experimenting with alcohol, you may be one of these people. Then again, you may be trying to convince yourself that your problem isn't that bad, that you don't really need help. There's really only one way to be sure: be completely honest with yourself.

DO I REALLY HAVE A PROBLEM?

If your behavior is ever a problem when you're drinking, if you act out in ways that are inappropriate or get into trouble or do things you later can't remember, you very clearly have a problem with drinking. Not all the signs of alcohol abuse, however, are quite so obvious. You may not do any of those things and yet still be an alcoholic or problem drinker. Since drinking problems tend to get worse over time rather than better, it is important to catch and stop any problem as early as possible.

Take a look at the following questions. The first four concern your possible genetic and/or biological tendency toward alcoholism. These are things that you can't do anything about. The other nine questions address the way you have learned to drink—behavior patterns that have become established over time. Whether you learned to do these things from your parents or your friends, or through your own experience, there is no reason to feel guilty about any of them. No one sets out to become an alcoholic, but given the right set of circumstances, it can happen to anyone.

1. *Are one or both of your parents alcoholic?*

   If one parent is an alcoholic, you stand a one-in-three chance of becoming an alcoholic yourself. If both parents are alcoholic, your chances are one-in-two.

2. *Are any of your grandparents or other relatives alcoholics?*

   Alcoholism tends to run in families. It can also skip a generation. The more alcoholics there are in your family, the higher your risk of becoming one yourself.

3. *Does alcohol seem to affect you more than it does other people? That is, does it make you feel really good or really high?*

   Different people react differently to alcohol. Some people get sick from just one drink. It is almost impossible for them to become alcoholics, because they literally can't "stomach" enough alcohol to get drunk. Other people experience intense and powerful feelings of euphoria. Their biological make-up makes them more susceptible to excessive drinking.

If you drink so much that you can't control your physical reactions and become drunk every time you indulge, then you probably have a problem with alcohol.

4. *Are you the kind of person who can really "hold your liquor?" Are you able to drink more than others? Has this been true since you first began drinking?*

Just as some people experience a stronger high from alcohol than others, some people tend to drink more. Even though they may not appear to have a drinking problem, however, the amount of alcohol they consume becomes a problem in and of itself. The body begins to physically need alcohol to function.

5. *Do you drink often? How often?*

Even though recent research shows that one or two drinks a day may actually be healthy for most adults, daily drinking is probably a sign of alcohol dependence. Most experts agree that as few as three drinks per day definitely increase a person's risk of developing heart disease as well as stomach, liver, colon, and other cancers. Five or more drinks per day is a sign of a serious alcohol problem and an indicator that the person may already be physically addicted.

The pattern of drinking every day slowly becomes a habit. Eventually, it becomes impossible to skip a day without feeling anxious or deprived. The amount of drinking generally increases. This type of drinker will become addicted, even though they may never feel drunk.

All drinking, even just one or two drinks a month, causes at least some damage to the body and may increase the risk of certain cancers and other diseases.

6. *Do you smoke cigarettes?*

Smoking cigarettes, drinking large amounts of coffee or soda, binging on junk food, or using drugs like marijuana, cocaine, and speed are all signs of compulsive or addictive behavior. These practices may indicate an addictive personality. Being a "shopaholic" (someone who likes to shop and spend money all the time), or a "workaholic," or a "chocoholic" (a person who constantly craves chocolate) may also be a sign of an addictive personality. This type of behavior puts a person at greater risk for becoming addicted to alcohol as well.

7. *Do you think about drinking a lot?*

It is only natural to wonder about what it's like to drink, but if you think about drinking all the time or find yourself frequently thinking about when, where, and how you can get a drink, you are showing signs of an obsession with alcohol—a major component of alcohol addiction. If you ever feel that you really "need" a drink, you may already be addicted.

8. *Do you drink to relax or forget your problems?*

When drinking becomes a part of your other problems or when you drink as a way of coping with those problems, then you also have a drinking problem. You may or may not be addicted at this point, but if you continue to use alcohol as a means of dealing with other problems in your life, you definitely will become addicted. Drinking as a means of coping with problems is problem drinking.

9. *Do you try to hide your drinking?*

Teenagers in the United States are forced to hide their drinking, since drinking is illegal for those under age 21. But trying to hide drinking, or lying about how much you've had to drink, virtually guarantees that you have a problem with alcohol.

The problem may be that you're afraid of being caught. Are you afraid because you think you'll get in trouble? Is what you're doing wrong? Even if you don't think it's wrong, you know that other people do. Whether you realize it or not, you feel guilty about your drinking.

This is part of the vicious cycle discussed earlier in the book. Feelings of guilt go away when you're drunk (and come back when you're sober), so you drink more to rid yourself of guilt. You deny that you have a drinking problem; the problem is that your parents would be angry if they knew you drank. You manage to drive yourself home from a party and sneak into your room without anyone knowing you're drunk. The fact that you made it home in one piece "proves" you weren't that drunk in the first place. You have just exhibited all of the major psychological symptoms of alcohol addiction.

10. *Do you ever drink alone?*

Drinking alone is a major hallmark of an alcohol problem. People who drink alone generally do so as a means of hiding their drinking or escaping their problems. They may drink alone because they feel they have no friends, because they feel sorry for themselves, or because they are bored. If you answered "yes" to this question, ask yourself why you drink alone. If you answer yourself honestly, you'll probably see that your reasons are the kind that will set you up to develop a drinking problem.

11. *Do you drink more than you used to?*

Alcoholism is a progressive condition. Over time, an alcoholic drinks more and more. If you used to drink a beer or two at a party, then later started drinking two or three, and recently have been drinking three, four, five, or more, you are exhibiting signs of progression in your drinking. Also, if you drink more frequently, you are showing signs of developing a problem with alcohol.

12. *Do you feel you "need" to drink to be comfortable with others?*

An inability to function in social situations without a drink is a sure sign of alcohol dependence. Drinking has taken the place of the social skills you once knew—or could have learned—before you started to drink.

13. *Do you ever get more drunk than you want to?*

Not being able to control your drinking, getting more drunk than you thought you were going to, telling yourself you're only going to have one drink and then having more than one, are all signs of alcohol dependence. The alcohol is in charge of you instead of you being in charge of it.

Go through the list again. Check off the ones that apply to you. Be honest. If you answered "yes" to any of these questions, you are at risk for developing a drinking problem. If you answered "yes" to three or more, you already have a problem with alcohol. You may be able to correct it on your own by changing your behavior and your relationship with alcohol, or you may not. If you answered "yes" to six or more, you have a serious problem with alcohol and need to get help immediately.

WHAT SHOULD I DO?

The first thing you need to do is talk to someone, preferably an adult trained in handling alcohol-related problems. If you have a good relationship with your parents, you may want to talk to them first. If that makes you too uncomfortable,

If you know that you have a drinking problem, talk to someone you trust. Don't continue to drink alone and hide your problem. You can get help.

or your parents are alcoholics, then find another adult who can help you ask them to talk to your parents with you. Why an adult? Because your friends may not know what to do. They may try to convince you that you don't really have a problem. They may be scared or have a problem too and don't want to admit it. If you are afraid to talk to your parents because they will become upset and punish you, talking to another adult can help ease those fears. If your parents also have a drinking problem or don't understand what alcoholism is, then they may not be able to give you the encouragement and support that you need right now.

If you have an adult relative you feel you can trust, try talking to him or her. Or talk to a social worker, counselor, a favorite teacher, or your minister, priest, or rabbi. If you are too embarrassed to talk with someone you know, call AA or one of the other organizations listed at the back of this book, and ask to talk to someone about drinking. The important thing is to take a first step and talk to someone.

The second step is to become involved in a structured program that will help you deal with your drinking. It costs nothing to join AA, and you will probably be surprised to see how many other people there are in the world who are just like you. "I was amazed at how many kids were there who were my age," remembers Jennifer about her first AA meeting. "And they all seemed so together and happy now that they were sober."

Some people who are physically addicted need to undergo detoxification at a hospital or medical treatment facility. Most people who require such severe intervention usually have more than one addiction. Young people in general haven't been drinking long enough to develop the kind of physical addiction that can lead to such serious withdrawal symptoms as violent physical tremors or hallucinations. Increasingly, however, more teens are being admitted to "detox" centers.

Whether you join AA, enter a treatment facility, or try a program like Rational Recovery (an alternative to AA), each will provide you with the support network you need to get through these difficult first few months. Almost all problem drinkers find they can't solve their problem alone. They need other understanding people to help keep them on track and let them know they are doing the right thing.

The early stages of quitting are the hardest. Both your mind and body will try to convince you to take a drink. It will be almost impossible to resist these forces alone, but you can do it with help. The first few weeks are so critical, that at AA, new members are asked to attend between five and seven meetings each week for the first month. People who know what you're going through, people who have been there themselves, will make themselves available and help you get through the tough times. Don't get upset or angry with yourself if you have a relapse. Many people do. It doesn't mean that you are weak or sick, it's just a sign of how strong your addiction to alcohol is, and how important it is for you to keep trying. You can do it, if you just take it one day at a time.

Jennifer finally made it on her second try. "What an incredible feeling of freedom it was," she says, "to get through that first day without any drugs or alcohol." "One day at a time" is one of the mottos of AA. Even Jason, who stopped drinking through a different program, got through the first weeks this way. He broke his addiction by turning it into a game he played with himself: "winning" the game when he made it through the first week, then "winning" again when he made it through the second. It has been nearly three years now since he had his last drink, and the powerful urges and cravings he used to feel are gone. "I'm the one who's in control now, not the booze," he says proudly.

RESPONSIBLE DRINKING

For some people, the only form of responsible drinking is no drinking at all. Even those experts who believe it is possible for some problem drinkers to learn how to drink responsibly think that there are people who should never drink. People who either have addictive personalities or who have had a serious addiction problem with alcohol or another drug are unlikely to ever be able to drink successfully. For them, abstinence—avoiding alcohol completely—is the

If you decide to drink, be sure that you recognize your own body's tolerance for alcohol, and how to avoid alcohol problems.

best and wisest policy. Most people, however, don't fall into this category—at least, not right away. How can you make sure that drinking will never become a problem for you?

For starters, wait until you are older. The earlier in life a person starts to drink, the more likely he or she is to develop a problem. Also, because underage drinking is illegal, teens who drink are often forced into the same behavior patterns practiced by alcoholics: sneaking drinks, lying about drinking, driving while under the influence. These are patterns you may not be able to break later in life.

It is also important for young people to learn social skills and gain self-confidence before they begin drinking. Alcohol only interferes with your ability to really learn how to talk to a girl or boy you like, ask that special someone to dance, or participate in a party game.

If and when you do decide to drink, treat alcohol with respect. See it as a food, not a drug. You probably wouldn't think of eating a whole pie every day or stuffing your face with french fries morning, noon, and night. That wouldn't be healthy. Think about drinking in the same way. Here are a few practical tips from the experts to help make sure drinking never becomes a problem for you.

Make your first drink a nonalcoholic one.

Most people down their first drink quickly. Drinking a nonalcoholic drink first will help you quench your thirst and kill the urge to "gulp" your drinks.

Always eat before you drink.

A full stomach doesn't prevent you from getting drunk, but it does help slow down the rate at which alcohol enters your bloodstream.

Always eat something with your drink.

This, too, will help slow the rate at which alcohol enters the bloodstream, and it will help keep you from finishing a drink too quickly. Salty foods like pretzels or potato chips should be avoided. The reason these are served free in bars is because they make people thirsty.

Alternate alcoholic and nonalcoholic drinks.

This trick does several things. First, it slows down the rate at which alcohol enters your system, and allows your body more time to absorb and dispose of the alcohol you've already had. Second, it reduces the total amount of alcohol you are likely to take in. Third, it psychologically reinforces the knowledge that you can have a good time even when you aren't drinking alcohol.

Drink in moderation.

For teens, this should mean no more than one or two drinks per month. This may not sound like very much, but if you feel the need for more, you probably already have a problem. As an adult you may enjoy an occasional glass of wine or beer with your meal, but don't drink every time alcohol is available. If you do, you will come to associate drinking alcohol as a necessary part of socializing.

Never drink and drive.

You don't have to feel "drunk" in order to put your ability to drive in jeopardy. The only responsible way for a teenager to drive is sober, so skip drinking altogether if you are driving. Offer to be a driver for others who drink. If you do drink after having driven, don't get behind the wheel again. Find another way home.

Here's another tip. Sign the SADD Contract for Life with your parents, and keep the lines of communication open, so that if you ever find yourself in a situation where you can't get home, you'll know your parents will be there to help. Lastly, never drink to escape your problems or because you feel unhappy. Only drink when you are in a good mood, and then always in moderation and as a part of your other activities, not as an end in itself.

CONTRACT FOR LIFE

MIDDLE SCHOOL SADD
STUDENTS AGAINST DOING DRUGS
A Contract for Life Between Parent and Middle School Student

Middle School Student: I agree to learn as much as possible about the effects of illegal substances, to share with you my concerns about peer pressure and to discuss these issues openly with you. I will contact you immediately for advice and guidance if I ever find myself in a situation where illegal substances are present. Under this contract I make a commitment to you not to use illegal substances. I also agree that I will not accept a ride with anyone who has been under the influence of drugs or alcohol.

_____
Signature

Parent: I will seek information and educate myself about realities of illegal substances. I agree to be an ever available resource for advice and communication with you. I agree that I will not use illegal substances. I also agree to seek safe, sober transportation home if I am ever in a situation where I have had too much to drink or a friend who is driving me has had too much to drink.

_____
Signature

_____
Date

SADD requires all young people to eliminate Alcohol and other Drugs from their lives.

Distributed by S.A.D.D. ''Students Against Driving Drunk''

Students Against Drunk Driving (SADD) has created this "Contract for Life" that young people and their parents can sign. See the back of this book for the SADD address to obtain a copy of the contract.

ADDITIONAL RESOURCES

Here is a list of agencies to contact for further information and program enrollment.

Addiction Alternatives, 1851 East First Street, Santa Ana, CA 92705.

Al-Anon Family Group Headquarters, Midtown Station, Box 862, New York, NY 10018 (800) 356-9996. Al-Anon was formed to help the families of alcoholics. They also have a program, **Alateen**, designed specifically to meet the needs of teenagers who come from families with alcoholics.

Alcoholics Anonymous (AA), P.O. Box 459, Grand Central Station, New York, NY 10163 (212) 870-3400. Local listings for AA are also available through directory information. Just dial 411.

Center for Substance Abuse Prevention/National Clearinghouse for Alcohol & Drug Information, P.O. Box 234, Rockville, MD 20847 (800) 729-6686.

Children of Alcoholics Foundation, 200 Park Avenue, 31st Floor, New York, NY 10166 (212) 351-2680.

Co-Dependents Anonymous, P.O. Box 33577, Phoenix, AZ 85067 (602) 277-7991.

Institute on Black Chemical Abuse, 261 Nicollet Avenue, Minneapolis, MN 55408.

Mothers Against Drunk Driving (MADD), P.O. Box 541688, Dallas, TX 75354 (214) 744-6233. MADD has several local chapters as well; call directory information in your area for a listing.

National Association for Children of Alcoholics (NACoA), 11426 Rockville Pike, Suite 100, Rockville, MD 20852 (301) 468-0985.

National Association for Native American Children of Alcoholics, 26 Round Butte Road, West Ronan, MT 59864 (406) 676-2500.

National Black Alcoholism Council, Inc. 1629 K Street NW, Suite 802, Washington, DC 20006 (202) 296-2696.

National Council on Alcohol and Drug Dependence (NCADD), 12 West 21st Street, New York, NY 10010 (212) 206-6770.

National Self-Help Clearinghouse, 25 West 43rd Street, Room 620, New York, NY 10036 (212) 642-2944. The Clearinghouse does not provide counseling services; instead they provide information about alcoholism. They prefer that people write rather than call. If you enclose a self-addressed stamped envelope along with your request for information about alcoholism, they will send you a list of the information they can provide.

Rational Recovery Systems, Box 800, Lotus, California 95651 (916) 621-4374. Rational Recovery is a program designed for people who find certain aspects of Alcoholics Anonymous to be incompatible with their beliefs. Many people who are uncomfortable with the religious aspects of AA find they are more at home with the nonspiritual, or "rational" approach of RR. Also, RR views alcoholism as a dependence and rejects labeling people alcoholics. They believe it is possible for some people who have had a drinking problem to learn to drink properly. AA insists that alcoholism is a disease, one for which there is no cure except total abstinence.

Students Against Drunk Driving (SADD), 200 Pleasant Street, Marlboro, MA 01752 (508) 481-3568.

Suzanne Somers Institute, 340 South Farrel Drive, Suite 203, Palm Springs, CA 92262 (619) 325-0110.

FOR FURTHER READING

Al-Anon Family Group. *Alateen: Hope for Children of Alcoholics.* New York, NY: Al-Anon Family Group Headquarters, 1981.

Bradshaw, John. *Homecoming.* New York, NY: Bantam, 1992.

Claypool, Jane. *Alcohol and You.* New York, NY: Franklin Watts, 1988.

Goodwin, Donald. *Is Alcoholism Hereditary?* 2nd ed. New York, NY: Ballantine, 1988.

Graeber, Laurel. *Are You Dying for a Drink?* New York, NY: Messner, 1985.

Hyde, Margaret O. *Alcohol: Drink or Drug?* New York, NY: McGraw-Hill, 1985.

Kinney, Jean and Gwen Leaton. *A Handbook of Alcohol Information.* St.Louis, MO; Mosby, 1978.

O'Brien, Robert and Morris Chafetz. *The Encyclopedia of Alcoholism.* New York, NY: Facts-On-File, 1982.

Silverstein, Alvin and Virginia B. *Alcoholism.* Philadelphia, PA: J. P. Lippincott, 1975.

Skynner, Robin and John Cleese. *Families and How to Survive Them.* New York, NY: Oxford University Press, 1983.

Vaillant, George. *The Natural History of Alcoholism.* Cambridge, MA: Harvard University Press, 1983.

Vogler, Roger E. and Wayne R. Bartz. *Teenagers and Alcohol: When Saying No Isn't Enough.* Philadelphia, PA: The Charles Press, 1992.

GLOSSARY

Abstinence. The voluntary refusal to drink alcoholic beverages.

Acting out. Behavior that is socially unacceptable, especially sexual behavior or physical violence.

Addiction. An irresistible and overwhelming dependence upon a substance.

Alcohol abuse. The immoderate or excessive consumption of alcohol (more than one or two drinks per day for adults; more than one or two drinks per month for teens). Any drinking that results in a person getting drunk is alcohol abuse.

Alcohol poisoning. A condition that occurs when too much alcohol gets into the bloodstream (0.40 percent or more), characterized by prolonged unconsciousness, brain damage, and even death.

Alcoholics Anonymous (AA). A nonprofit organization dedicated to helping people stop drinking.

Alcoholism. The disease or condition characterized by addiction to alcohol. Alcoholism is a chronic dependence on alcohol that tends to get worse over time if not treated.

Anesthesia, anesthetic. Any substance that significantly reduces or eliminates the sensation of pain. Loss of consciousness may or may not occur.

Atrophy. A loss of cells or wasting away of body tissue, especially muscles. Chronic alcohol abuse can result in damage to brain and muscle cells as well as to other organs, especially those involved in digestion (liver, stomach, pancreas, intestines).

Blood alcohol content (BAC). The percentage of alcohol present in the bloodstream.

Cirrhosis. A disease of the liver characterized by massive scarring and hardening, as well as by a marked decrease in function. While it is not neccessary for someone to be an alcoholic to get cirrhosis, alcoholics stand a greater chance of developing the disease, and even moderate consumption of alcohol may increase a person's risk.

Co-dependent, co-dependency. When someone organizes his or her behavior around that of an addict of any kind, that person is co-dependent. The co-dependent derives his or her own sense of worth from taking care of the addict. A co-dependent is most often the spouse or a child.

Denial. The refusal to admit that a problem exists. Alcoholics are frequently in a state of denial about their situation. Their families and friends may also be in denial.

Designated driver. A person who agrees not to drink and provides others who do drink with rides to and from a party/restaurant/bar.

Distillation. The process of boiling a liquid, then collecting and recondensing the vapors that are produced. Certain types of alcohol are distilled as a way of increasing their alcohol content.

Dysfunctional families. Families in which the parents are either absent or not fulfilling their duties as parents. When a parent drinks too much, he or she is not capable of being a good parent. The resulting imbalance in the family often creates serious emotional and psychological problems for the children.

Euphoria. A feeling of vigor, well-being, or high spirits.

Ethyl alcohol. A naturally occurring byproduct of fermentation when yeast is present in a liquid that contains sugar. All alcoholic beverages such as beer, wine, and hard liquor, contain ethyl alcohol.

Fermentation. The process by which alcoholic beverages are produced. Live, active yeast present in a given liquid (such as grape juice) eats the sugar and cabohydrates, and excretes the ethyl alcohol that gives liquor its "kick."

Fortification. The process of adding more ethyl alcohol to a liquor after its natural fermentation has stopped.

Genetic predisposition. A tendency to develop a certain trait, characteristic, or disease based on one's biological history or heredity.

Hangover. The feelings of nausea, vomiting, headache, and dry mouth that often follow a day or night of heavy drinking.

Heredity. The traits or characteristics a person inherits from his or her ancestors, such as eye or hair color. There is evidence that an increased risk of developing certain diseases and/or conditions, including diabetes, heart disease, and alcoholism, can be inherited.

Intervention. During an intervention, an alcoholic's family and friends confront the person with the facts about their drinking and encourage him or her to seek professional treatment. An intervention is designed not to embarrass the drinker, but rather to assist him in facing up to the fact that he has a problem and needs to get help.

Moderation. With respect to alcohol consumption, moderation is considered to be no more than one or two drinks per day for adults, and no more than one or two drinks per month for older teens approaching adulthood.

Progressive condition. One that gets steadily worse over time. Alcoholism is a progressive condition.

Proof. A number equal to two times the amount of alcohol present in certain types of liquor, especially distilled liquors. It derives from an ancient system that allowed distillers to "prove" how strong their liquor was.

Psychomotor skills. The combination of a person's mental and emotional thoughts and judgments (psycho) and their physical reactions (motor). Alcohol adversely affects all of a person's psychomotor skills.

Rebound effect. A side effect of all sedatives. Several hours after the depressant effects of a sedative wear off, they are replaced by an increase, or "rebound" in brain and nervous system activity. This rebound can heighten a person's sense of tension or anxiety.

Sedative. Any of a group of drugs, including alcohol, which act to depress or calm nervous system activity.

Self-esteem. The way in which a person views him or herself. People with high self-esteem like themselves; people with low self-esteem do not. Many alcoholics suffer from low self-esteem.

Tolerance. In this case, a person's ability to "hold their liquor." Someone who appears very drunk after only one drink has a low tolerance for alcohol. While we often praise people for having a high tolerance for alcohol, the higher a person's tolerance, the greater the risk they run for developing an alcohol-related problem.

Withdrawal. The symptoms some people experience when their supply of alcohol (or other drug) is suddenly shut off. These symptoms include tremors, nausea, excessive sweating, muscle cramps, vomiting, explosive emotional outbursts, diarrhea, and dizziness. In severe cases, sudden withdrawal from alcohol can produce hallucinations and even death.

INDEX

D

denial (of alcoholism), 9, 44, 55-57, 67, 77
depressant, 23, 27
drinking
    for acceptance, 38
    alone, 82
    and death rate, 27
    and driving, 16, 28-29, 38, 44-45, 73, 75
    hidden, 60, 73, 80, 85
    historic references to, 40
    and humor, 19
    and legal drinking age, 16, 44, 73, 80
    in moderation, 25, 27, 40, 87
    and mood swings, 32-33, 34, 73
    and other cultures, 17
    parents who encourage, 21, 35, 43, 53
    responsibly, 17, 78, 85-87
    and socializing, 16, 27-29, 34, 53, 59, 73, 85
    and sports, 16
    on television, 19
drinks (servings), 23
drunk(s)
    "happy," 33, 35
    "hollow leg," 41
    "mean," 33
    "one drink," 41
drunkenness, 16, 19, 40, 59, 60, 71, 73, 82, 83
DUI (Driving Under the Influence), 29, 38, 45

E

ethyl alcohol, 22

F

fermentation, 22
fetal alcohol syndrome, 66

G

Goodwin, Donald, Dr., 52, 53

H

"Happy Hour," 16
HDL ("good" cholesterol), 27

I

intervention, 68-69
isopropyl alcohol, 22

K

Kern, Dr. Marc, 16, 35, 67

L

liquor (distilled), 23

M

MADD (Mothers Against Drunk Driving), 16

N

National Association for Children of Alcoholics (NACoA), 64, 65
National Council on Alcoholism, 9
National Council on Alcoholism and Drug Dependency (NCADD), 40-41, 50, 55
Noah, 40

O

Old Testament, 40

P

parents who drink, 11, 14, 16, 25, 34, 35, 43, 52-53, 53-55, 63-69, 78
placebo effect, 28

R

Rational Recovery, 84
rebound effect, 24-25, 25 (chart), 32
Reye's Syndrome, 27
rubbing (isopropyl) alcohol, 22

S

T

V